Quietness

Unlock the Power of Quietness: Embrace Solitude, Find Inner Peace, and Transform Your Life with the Proven Strategies and Insights of Quietness - The Ultimate Guide to Self-Discovery, Personal Growth, and Lasting Happiness!

Lance P. Richards

Quietness: Unlock the Power of Quietness: Embrace Solitude, Find Inner Peace, and Transform Your Life with the Proven Strategies and Insights of Quietness - The Ultimate Guide to Self-Discovery, Personal Growth, and Lasting Happiness!

Table of Contents

01: The Power of Quietness: An Introduction

The modern world is a cacophony of noise. From the constant hum of traffic and the endless stream of notifications on our devices, to the chatter of coworkers and the blare of television sets, there seems to be no escaping the constant barrage of sound that surrounds us. In this frenzied environment, it can be easy to lose sight of the value of quietness, and the profound impact it can have on our lives.

But what if we were to embrace silence, and learn to find peace in the absence of sound? What if we were to make space for quietness in our lives, and allow it to guide us on a journey of self-discovery and personal growth? In this chapter, we'll explore the power of quietness, and discover how it can help us to unlock our full potential, find inner peace, and transform our lives in profound ways.

To understand the power of quietness, we must first explore what it means to be quiet. At its core, quietness is not simply the absence of noise, but a state of mind characterized by stillness, calm, and introspection. It is a state of being in which we are fully present, aware of ourselves and our surroundings, and at peace with the world around us.

01: THE POWER OF QUIETNESS: AN INTRODUCTION

For many of us, the idea of being quiet may seem daunting, even uncomfortable. We may associate silence with loneliness, or feel that we need constant stimulation to stay engaged with the world around us. But the truth is, quietness can be a source of great strength and resilience, helping us to cultivate a deeper sense of self-awareness, compassion, and understanding.

In fact, some of history's greatest thinkers and leaders were known for their love of quietness. From Buddha, who sought enlightenment through meditation and introspection, to Mahatma Gandhi, who spent hours each day in silent contemplation, these figures recognized the transformative power of stillness and quietness.

So how can we begin to embrace quietness in our own lives? One of the first steps is simply to make space for it. This may mean carving out time each day for meditation, or simply taking a few moments to sit quietly and breathe deeply, allowing ourselves to become fully present in the moment.

Another key aspect of embracing quietness is learning to let go of the distractions and noise that can so easily pull us away from our inner selves. This may mean unplugging from technology, spending time in nature, or simply taking a break from the demands of our daily lives to reflect and recharge.

Ultimately, the power of quietness lies in its ability to help us connect with our deepest selves, and tap into the wisdom and insight that lies within. By embracing stillness and introspection, we can find greater clarity and purpose, and cultivate a sense of inner peace that will sustain us through even the most challenging times.

In the chapters that follow, we'll explore a range of strategies and insights for embracing quietness in our lives, from the power of meditation and mindfulness, to the transformative potential of solitude and introspection. By the end of this book, you'll have the tools and knowledge you need to unlock the full power of quietness, and transform your life in ways you never thought possible. So let's dive in, and discover the power of stillness, calm, and introspection together!

02: Quietness and the Modern World

In today's modern world, we are constantly bombarded with noise, distractions, and stimuli. From the sound of traffic on the streets, to the constant notifications on our smartphones, to the endless stream of news and information that floods our screens, it can feel impossible to find a moment of peace and quiet.

But the truth is, quietness is more important than ever in our fast-paced and chaotic world. In fact, it is essential to our physical, mental, and emotional well-being. In this chapter, we will explore the benefits of quietness in the modern world, and look at some of the challenges we face in finding it.

One of the most significant benefits of quietness is its ability to reduce stress and anxiety. When we are constantly surrounded by noise and stimuli, our bodies go into a state of high alert, triggering the release of stress hormones like cortisol and adrenaline. Over time, this chronic stress can lead to a range of health problems, from cardiovascular disease to depression.

But when we embrace quietness, we allow our bodies and minds to relax and recharge. We give ourselves the space we need to process our thoughts and emotions, and to let go of the tension and anxiety that build up over time. This can have a profound impact on our overall health and well-being, improving everything from our sleep quality to our immune function.

In addition to its physical benefits, quietness is also essential for our mental and emotional health. In a world where we are constantly connected to others through social media, email, and messaging apps, it can be easy to feel overwhelmed and disconnected. But when we take the time to disconnect from the noise and distractions of modern life, we give ourselves the space we need to connect with our inner selves, to reflect on our thoughts and feelings, and to gain a deeper understanding of who we are.

This is particularly important for those of us who struggle with anxiety, depression, or other mental health challenges. By embracing quietness, we can develop the tools and strategies we need to manage our symptoms, and to cultivate a sense of inner peace and calm that can help us navigate even the most challenging times.

Of course, finding quietness in the modern world is easier said than done. We are surrounded by noise and distractions at every turn, and it can feel like there is never a moment of peace to be found. But with a few simple strategies and techniques, it is possible to unlock the power of quietness and transform your life.

One of the most effective strategies for finding quietness is to make it a priority in your daily routine. This might mean setting aside time each day for meditation, yoga, or other mindfulness practices that can help you connect with your inner self and cultivate a sense of calm. It might also mean carving out time for quiet reflection and introspection, whether that's through journaling, taking a long walk in nature, or simply sitting in silence for a few moments each day.

Another important strategy for finding quietness is to disconnect from technology and social media whenever possible. This might mean turning off your phone or computer during meals, setting boundaries around when and how you check your email or social media accounts, or even taking a digital detox from time to time to give yourself a break from the constant barrage of information and stimuli.

It is also important to cultivate a physical environment that supports quietness. This might mean creating a dedicated space in your home where you can go to meditate or practice yoga, or it might mean investing in noise-cancelling headphones or soundproofing your living space to reduce the impact of outside noise.

Ultimately, the key to unlocking the power of quietness in the modern world is to make it a priority in your life. By embracing the benefits of quietness, and by developing the strategies and tools you need to cultivate it, you can transform your life in countless ways. You might find that you are better able to manage stress and anxiety, that you are more connected to your inner self and your emotions, and that you are able to approach challenges with greater clarity and focus.

Of course, there will always be challenges and obstacles that stand in the way of finding quietness in the modern world. But by approaching these challenges with a spirit of curiosity and openness, and by continuing to prioritize quietness in your life, you can continue to unlock its transformative power and experience all of the benefits it has to offer.

One of the biggest challenges that many people face when it comes to finding quietness in the modern world is the pressure to constantly be "on." Whether it's responding to emails or text messages at all hours of the day and night, or feeling like you need to constantly be connected to social media and news sites to stay informed, it can be difficult to unplug and disconnect from the world around you.

But the truth is, you don't need to be constantly "on" to be successful or productive in your life. In fact, taking the time to step back and disconnect can be just as important as staying connected and engaged. By prioritizing quietness, you can give yourself the space you need to recharge and refocus, so that you can approach your work and your relationships with renewed energy and clarity.

Another challenge that many people face when it comes to finding quietness is the sense of guilt or shame that can arise when you take time for yourself. Whether it's the feeling that you should always be doing more, or the sense that taking time for yourself is somehow selfish or indulgent, these feelings can make it difficult to prioritize quietness in your life.

But the truth is, taking time for yourself is not selfish or indulgent - it's essential to your well-being. When you prioritize quietness, you are not only taking care of yourself, but you are also creating a foundation for success and happiness in all areas of your life. By investing in yourself and your well-being, you are able to show up more fully and authentically in your relationships and your work, and to approach each day with renewed energy and purpose.

In the end, the key to unlocking the power of quietness in the modern world is to approach it with a spirit of curiosity and openness, and to be willing to experiment with different strategies and techniques to find what works best for you. Whether it's carving out time for daily meditation, taking a digital detox, or simply spending more time in nature, there are countless ways to cultivate quietness in your life and to experience all of the benefits it has to offer.

So if you're feeling overwhelmed or disconnected in your life, take a moment to reflect on the power of quietness, and consider how you can make it a priority in your daily routine. Whether you're looking to reduce stress and anxiety, deepen your connections with others, or simply find greater peace and happiness in your life, embracing the power of quietness can help you transform your life in ways you never thought possible.

03: The Science of Quietness: What Research Shows

Introduction

In a world that values constant activity and noise, quietness can seem like a luxury. But research shows that quietness is essential to our well-being. It has been shown to reduce stress, improve creativity, and even enhance physical health. In this chapter, we will explore the science of quietness, examining the research on its benefits and exploring how we can incorporate more quietness into our lives.

The Benefits of Quietness

There are many benefits to incorporating more quietness into our lives. Let's explore some of the most significant:

Reduced Stress

In a world where we are bombarded with constant noise and stimulation, it's no surprise that stress levels are on the rise. But research shows that spending time in quietness can help reduce stress levels. One study found that just two minutes of silence can reduce blood pressure and heart rate, two key indicators of stress.

03: THE SCIENCE OF QUIETNESS: WHAT RESEARCH SHOWS

Improved Creativity

When we are surrounded by noise and activity, it can be difficult to tap into our creativity. But research shows that quietness can help improve our creative thinking. A study published in the journal Psychological Science found that participants who were placed in a quiet environment were more likely to come up with creative solutions to problems than those who were in a noisy environment.

Enhanced Physical Health

Quietness can also have physical health benefits. One study found that people who spent time in nature, which tends to be quiet, had lower levels of the stress hormone cortisol and improved immune system function. Another study found that people who meditated in quiet environments had lower levels of inflammation, which is linked to a range of chronic health conditions.

Improved Sleep

Sleep is essential to our overall health and well-being, but many of us struggle to get enough quality sleep. Quietness can help improve our sleep by reducing the level of external stimuli that can disrupt our sleep cycles. A study published in the journal Sleep Medicine found that participants who were exposed to noise during sleep had lower sleep quality and were more likely to wake up feeling tired.

How to Incorporate More Quietness into Your Life

Now that we've explored the benefits of quietness, let's look at some strategies for incorporating more of it into our lives:

Take Quiet Breaks

One of the simplest ways to incorporate more quietness into your life is to take quiet breaks throughout the day. This could be as simple as taking a few minutes to sit quietly in a park or even just closing your eyes and taking a few deep breaths. These breaks can help reduce stress and improve focus.

Find a Quiet Space

If you're finding it challenging to find quietness in your daily life, consider creating a dedicated quiet space in your home. This could be a corner of a room or even a separate room entirely. Make it a space where you can disconnect from the noise and activity of daily life and focus on quietness.

Try Meditation

Meditation is a powerful tool for cultivating quietness. It involves sitting quietly and focusing your attention on your breath or a specific object. Meditation has been shown to reduce stress, improve focus, and enhance creativity. Even just a few minutes of meditation per day can have significant benefits.

Get Outside

Spending time in nature is a great way to incorporate more quietness into your life. Whether it's taking a walk in the park or hiking in the woods, being in nature can help reduce stress and improve your overall sense of well-being.

Limit Screen Time

The constant noise and stimulation of screens can make it challenging to find quietness in our lives. Consider setting

aside specific times of the day to disconnect from screens
and focus on quietness. This could be as simple as turning
off your phone during meals or setting a specific time each
day to read a book or listen to music in a quiet space.

Practice Mindfulness

Mindfulness is the practice of being present and fully engaged in the current moment. By focusing on the present
moment and paying attention to our thoughts and emotions, we can cultivate a sense of quietness and inner peace.
Mindfulness can be practiced in a variety of ways, including
meditation, yoga, and even just taking a few deep breaths
throughout the day.

Embrace Solitude

Many of us are uncomfortable with the idea of being alone,
but solitude can be a powerful tool for cultivating quietness
and self-awareness. Try spending some time alone each day,
even if it's just a few minutes. This can be a time to reflect
on your thoughts and emotions and reconnect with yourself.

Conclusion

03: THE SCIENCE OF QUIETNESS: WHAT RESEARCH SHOWS

Quietness is essential to our well-being, but in a world that values constant activity and noise, it can be challenging to find. By incorporating more quietness into our lives, we can reduce stress, improve creativity, and enhance our physical health. Whether it's taking quiet breaks throughout the day, finding a quiet space in your home, or practicing meditation, there are many strategies for cultivating quietness in our lives. By embracing quietness, we can unlock the power of solitude, find inner peace, and transform our lives.

04: The Benefits of Quietness: Mind, Body, and Soul

Quietness is not just an absence of noise. It is a state of being that has the power to transform our minds, bodies, and souls. In this chapter, we will explore the benefits of quietness in great detail, examining how it can improve our physical health, enhance our mental clarity, and nourish our spiritual well-being.

Physical Benefits of Quietness

First and foremost, quietness has a direct impact on our physical health. When we are constantly surrounded by noise, our bodies are forced to work harder to maintain equilibrium. This can lead to a range of negative health outcomes, including high blood pressure, cardiovascular disease, and increased levels of stress hormones like cortisol.

Conversely, studies have shown that quietness can have a positive impact on our physical health. For example, a study published in the Journal of Environmental Psychology found that exposure to natural sounds (like birds chirping or waves crashing) can lower blood pressure and reduce feelings of stress and anxiety.

Similarly, a study published in the journal Heart found that spending time in quiet natural environments (like forests or parks) can lower levels of the stress hormone cortisol, improve heart rate variability, and even lower the risk of cardiovascular disease.

In addition to these physical benefits, quietness can also improve our mental health in numerous ways.

Mental Benefits of Quietness

One of the most obvious benefits of quietness is improved mental clarity. When we are constantly bombarded by noise, our minds become scattered and distracted, making it difficult to focus on the task at hand. By contrast, when we are in a quiet environment, our minds can more easily focus and concentrate, leading to increased productivity and a greater sense of accomplishment.

Moreover, quietness can also be a powerful tool for reducing stress and anxiety. In fact, many people use meditation and other quiet practices as a way to manage their mental health. By quieting the mind and focusing on the present moment, we can cultivate a sense of inner peace and calm, which can help to reduce feelings of anxiety and overwhelm.

Quietness can also improve our relationships with others. When we are in a quiet environment, we are better able to listen and communicate with those around us, which can lead to deeper connections and more meaningful relationships.

Spiritual Benefits of Quietness

Finally, quietness can also have a profound impact on our spiritual well-being. When we take time to be quiet and still, we can connect with a deeper sense of meaning and purpose in our lives. This can be especially important for those who are searching for greater meaning and direction in their lives.

In addition, quietness can also help us to cultivate a greater sense of compassion and empathy for others. When we are quiet and still, we are more able to connect with the suffering of others and to feel a sense of shared humanity with all those around us.

Ultimately, the benefits of quietness are vast and far-reaching. From improved physical health to enhanced mental clarity and spiritual well-being, quietness has the power to transform our lives in countless ways. Whether through meditation, spending time in nature, or simply taking a few moments each day to be quiet and still, we can all benefit from the power of quietness in our lives.

05: Cultivating Quietness: Creating Space in Your Life

In today's fast-paced world, it's hard to find a moment of peace and quiet. We live in a culture that values constant activity and productivity, where we are always connected to technology and surrounded by noise. It's easy to become overwhelmed and stressed out, and this can have a negative impact on our mental and physical health. In this chapter, we will explore the concept of quietness and how it can transform your life. We will discuss the benefits of cultivating quietness, as well as practical strategies for creating space in your life.

What is Quietness?

Quietness is the state of being calm, still, and peaceful. It is a state of mind that is free from distraction and external noise. It's not just about physical silence, but also about finding a sense of inner stillness. Quietness is a powerful tool that can help us find clarity, reduce stress, and connect with our true selves.

The Benefits of Cultivating Quietness

05: CULTIVATING QUIETNESS: CREATING SPACE IN YOUR LIFE

Cultivating quietness has numerous benefits for our mental, emotional, and physical health. Here are just a few:

Reduced Stress and Anxiety: When we cultivate quietness, we are able to slow down and take a break from the constant stimulation of the world around us. This can help us reduce stress and anxiety, and find a sense of calm.

Increased Self-Awareness: When we create space in our lives for quietness, we are better able to connect with our inner selves. We become more aware of our thoughts, feelings, and behaviors, which can help us make positive changes in our lives.

Improved Focus and Productivity: When we are constantly bombarded by distractions, it can be hard to focus on the task at hand. Cultivating quietness can help us improve our focus and productivity, allowing us to accomplish more in less time.

Enhanced Creativity: Quietness can help us tap into our creativity and imagination. When we are free from distractions, we are able to think more deeply and come up with new ideas.

05: CULTIVATING QUIETNESS: CREATING SPACE IN YOUR LIFE

Improved Relationships: When we cultivate quietness, we are better able to communicate with others. We are more patient, understanding, and compassionate, which can lead to stronger relationships.

Practical Strategies for Creating Space in Your Life

Now that we understand the benefits of cultivating quietness, let's explore some practical strategies for creating space in your life.

Schedule Quiet Time: Make it a point to schedule quiet time into your daily routine. This could be as simple as taking a few minutes each morning to meditate or read a book.

Disconnect from Technology: Technology can be a major source of distraction and noise in our lives. Try disconnecting from technology for a set period of time each day, or setting aside specific times to check your phone or email.

Spend Time in Nature: Nature has a way of calming our minds and reducing stress. Make it a point to spend time outside each day, even if it's just a short walk around the block.

05: CULTIVATING QUIETNESS: CREATING SPACE IN YOUR LIFE

Practice Mindfulness: Mindfulness is the practice of being present and fully engaged in the moment. When we practice mindfulness, we are better able to focus and find a sense of calm.

Simplify Your Life: Simplifying your life can help you create more space for quietness. This could mean decluttering your home, simplifying your schedule, or letting go of commitments that no longer serve you.

Practice Gratitude: Gratitude is a powerful tool for cultivating a sense of peace and happiness. Take time each day to reflect on what you are grateful for, whether it's a beautiful sunset or the love of your family.

In conclusion, cultivating quietness is a powerful tool that can help us find inner peace, reduce stress, and transform our lives. By creating space in our lives for quietness, we can improve our relationships, increase our self-awareness, and enhance our creativity. It's important to remember that cultivating quietness is a journey, and it's okay to start small. By incorporating some of the strategies discussed in this chapter into your daily routine, you can begin to experience the benefits of quietness and transform your life.

05: CULTIVATING QUIETNESS: CREATING SPACE IN YOUR LIFE

One final strategy to consider when cultivating quietness is to surround yourself with supportive people. Finding a community of like-minded individuals who value stillness and quietness can help you stay motivated and inspired on your journey. This could mean joining a meditation group, attending a silent retreat, or simply connecting with friends who share your values.

In addition, it's important to remember that quietness looks different for everyone. Some people may find solace in sitting in silence, while others may prefer to engage in creative activities such as painting or writing. The key is to find what works for you and to create space in your life for the things that bring you peace and joy.

In conclusion, cultivating quietness is a powerful tool that can help us find inner peace, reduce stress, and transform our lives. By scheduling quiet time, disconnecting from technology, spending time in nature, practicing mindfulness, simplifying our lives, and practicing gratitude, we can create space in our lives for quietness and unlock its transformative power. Remember that quietness is a journey, and it's okay to start small. With time and practice, you can develop a deeper sense of calm and find lasting happiness.

06: Solitude and Silence: The Importance of Alone Time

In our modern world, we are constantly surrounded by noise and chaos. From the blaring horns of traffic to the constant barrage of emails and notifications, it can be hard to find a moment of peace and quiet. But despite the constant noise, there is immense value in solitude and silence. In fact, many of the world's greatest thinkers, artists, and innovators have embraced the power of solitude and used it to achieve great things.

In this chapter, we'll explore the importance of alone time, and the ways in which it can help you find inner peace, unlock your creativity, and transform your life. We'll delve into the science behind solitude, and examine some of the proven strategies and insights that can help you harness its power.

But first, let's take a closer look at what we mean by solitude and silence. Solitude refers to the state of being alone, and is often associated with feelings of loneliness or isolation. But in the context of this chapter, solitude refers to intentional alone time – a period of time when you deliberately separate yourself from others in order to reflect, recharge, and reconnect with yourself. Silence, on the other hand, refers to the absence of noise or sound, and can be experienced both internally and externally. Internal silence refers to a state of mental calm and stillness, while external silence refers to the absence of noise or distractions.

So why is solitude and silence so important? The answer lies in the fact that we live in a world that is increasingly noisy and distracting. Our attention is constantly being pulled in different directions, and we are bombarded with information and stimulation from all angles. This can be exhausting and overwhelming, and can leave us feeling drained and disconnected from ourselves. Solitude and silence provide an antidote to this constant stimulation, allowing us to step back from the noise and distractions of the world, and connect with ourselves on a deeper level.

In fact, research has shown that spending time in solitude and silence can have numerous benefits for our mental and physical health. Studies have found that solitude can help us regulate our emotions, reduce stress and anxiety, and improve our overall well-being. It can also help us tap into our creativity and imagination, and can lead to increased self-awareness and personal growth.

So how can you incorporate solitude and silence into your life? There are many different ways to do so, depending on your preferences and lifestyle. Here are a few ideas to get you started:

Take a solo walk: Going for a walk on your own can be a great way to clear your mind and connect with nature. Leave your phone at home, and allow yourself to simply be present in the moment.

Meditate: Meditation is a powerful tool for cultivating inner stillness and silence. Find a quiet place to sit and meditate for a few minutes each day, focusing on your breath and allowing your thoughts to come and go.

Disconnect from technology: Take a break from your phone, computer, and other electronic devices. Turn off notifications and set aside some time each day to disconnect and be fully present in the moment.

Journal: Writing can be a powerful tool for self-reflection and introspection. Set aside some time each day to write down your thoughts and feelings, without worrying about grammar or spelling.

Create: Engage in a creative activity that allows you to tap into your imagination and express yourself. This could be anything from drawing or painting to writing poetry or playing music.

Take a retreat: Consider taking a solo retreat or attending a silent meditation retreat. These can be powerful opportunities to step away from the distractions of daily life and connect with yourself on a deeper level.

Incorporating solitude and silence into your life may feel challenging at first, especially if you are used to constant stimulation and activity.

07: The Art of Listening: Deepening Your Connection with Others

We live in a world that is becoming increasingly noisy and distracting. The constant barrage of information and stimuli can be overwhelming, leaving us feeling disconnected and frazzled. However, amidst all this chaos, there is an art to listening – a skill that can be developed to deepen our connection with others and bring more quietness into our lives.

Listening is more than just hearing the words that someone is saying. It involves paying attention to the nuances of their tone, body language, and emotions. When we truly listen to someone, we open ourselves up to their experiences and perspectives, which can help us grow and learn.

In this chapter, we will explore the art of listening and how it can transform our relationships and our lives. We will discuss the barriers to effective listening and offer tips and techniques for becoming a better listener.

The Barriers to Effective Listening

Before we can become effective listeners, it is important to understand the barriers that can prevent us from truly hearing what someone is saying. These barriers can be internal or external and can include:

Distractions: We live in a world of constant distractions – smartphones, social media, email, and television. These distractions can prevent us from fully focusing on the person in front of us, making it difficult to truly listen to what they are saying.

Prejudices and biases: Our own prejudices and biases can prevent us from truly hearing what someone is saying. We may make assumptions about their experiences or perspectives based on our own biases, which can prevent us from fully understanding their point of view.

Judgments: We often listen with the intention of responding rather than understanding. We may make judgments about the person or their ideas before they have even finished speaking, which can prevent us from truly hearing what they are saying.

Emotional barriers: Our own emotions can prevent us from truly hearing what someone is saying. If we are feeling angry or upset, for example, we may not be able to fully focus on the person in front of us, making it difficult to truly listen to what they are saying.

Cultural differences: Cultural differences can make it difficult to truly understand what someone is saying. Different cultures may have different communication styles or may use different idioms or expressions, which can be confusing for someone who is not familiar with them.

Tips for Becoming a Better Listener

Now that we understand the barriers to effective listening, let's explore some tips and techniques for becoming a better listener. These techniques can help us deepen our connection with others and bring more quietness into our lives.

Be present: The first step to becoming a better listener is to be present. This means focusing all of our attention on the person in front of us and putting aside any distractions or preoccupations. By being fully present, we can create a safe and supportive space for the other person to express themselves.

Practice empathy: Empathy is the ability to put ourselves in someone else's shoes and understand their perspective. When we practice empathy, we can truly hear what someone is saying and connect with them on a deeper level. To practice empathy, we can try to imagine what it would be like to be in the other person's situation and validate their feelings and experiences.

Avoid interrupting: Interrupting someone when they are speaking can be disrespectful and can prevent us from truly hearing what they are saying. To become a better listener, we can practice avoiding interruptions and allow the other person to fully express themselves before responding.

Ask open-ended questions: Open-ended questions are questions that cannot be answered with a simple "yes" or "no". These questions can encourage the other person to share more about their experiences and perspectives, which can deepen our understanding of them.

Practice active listening: Active listening is a technique that involves fully engaging with the person who is speaking by using verbal and nonverbal cues to show that we are fully present and engaged. This can include nodding our heads, maintaining eye contact, and paraphrasing what the person has said to show that we are truly listening and understanding.

Be mindful of your own biases: It's important to be aware of our own biases and prejudices when we are listening to others. We can challenge our own assumptions and try to approach each conversation with an open mind and a willingness to learn.

Practice reflective listening: Reflective listening is a technique that involves summarizing what the person has said to ensure that we have understood their message correctly. This can help us avoid misunderstandings and ensure that we are truly hearing what the other person is saying.

Show empathy through body language: Our body language can communicate empathy and support. We can show that we are fully present and engaged by maintaining eye contact, nodding our heads, and using other nonverbal cues to show that we are actively listening and empathizing with the other person.

Practice active curiosity: Active curiosity involves asking questions and seeking to learn more about the other person's experiences and perspectives. By practicing active curiosity, we can deepen our understanding of others and build stronger, more meaningful relationships.

Practice self-reflection: Finally, it's important to practice self-reflection and examine our own listening habits and patterns. By reflecting on our own strengths and weaknesses as listeners, we can identify areas for growth and continue to improve our listening skills over time.

The Power of Listening

When we become better listeners, we can deepen our connection with others, build stronger relationships, and even transform our own lives. By truly hearing what someone else is saying, we can learn from their experiences, gain new perspectives, and grow in empathy and understanding.

In addition to improving our relationships with others, listening can also bring more quietness into our lives. When we focus all of our attention on the present moment and truly listen to those around us, we can experience a sense of calm and inner peace that can be difficult to find in our fast-paced, noisy world.

07: THE ART OF LISTENING: DEEPENING YOUR CONNECTION WITH OTHERS

Conclusion

In this chapter, we have explored the art of listening and how it can transform our relationships and our lives. By understanding the barriers to effective listening and practicing techniques for becoming a better listener, we can deepen our connection with others and experience more quietness in our lives.

Remember, listening is more than just hearing the words that someone is saying. It involves paying attention to the nuances of their tone, body language, and emotions. When we truly listen to someone, we open ourselves up to their experiences and perspectives, which can help us grow and learn. So, let's all strive to become better listeners and embrace the power of quietness in our lives.

08: Mindful Meditation: Quieting the Mind and Finding Peace

The mind is a powerful tool that can help us achieve great things. It can be the source of our creativity, innovation, and productivity. However, the mind can also be our greatest enemy, causing us to feel anxious, stressed, and overwhelmed. Mindful meditation is a technique that helps us quiet our minds and find peace. It is a practice that has been used for thousands of years to promote mental clarity, emotional stability, and spiritual growth. In this chapter, we will explore the benefits of mindful meditation and provide you with practical tips on how to incorporate it into your daily routine.

What is Mindful Meditation?

Mindful meditation is a practice of focusing on the present moment without judgment. It involves sitting in a quiet place, closing your eyes, and directing your attention to your breath or a specific object or sound. When you practice mindful meditation, you become aware of your thoughts, feelings, and sensations without reacting to them. This helps you gain a deeper understanding of your mind and emotions, and cultivate a sense of inner peace and calm.

08: MINDFUL MEDITATION: QUIETING THE MIND AND FINDING PEACE

The Benefits of Mindful Meditation

The benefits of mindful meditation are numerous and have been scientifically proven. Studies have shown that regular practice of mindful meditation can:

Reduce stress and anxiety: Mindful meditation helps reduce the production of stress hormones and activate the para-sympathetic nervous system, which promotes relaxation and reduces anxiety.

Improve emotional regulation: Mindful meditation helps you become more aware of your emotions and respond to them in a healthy and constructive way.

Boost creativity and innovation: Mindful meditation promotes the activation of the default mode network, which is responsible for creative and innovative thinking.

Enhance focus and attention: Mindful meditation increases the activity in the prefrontal cortex, which is responsible for focus and attention.

Promote physical health: Mindful meditation has been shown to reduce blood pressure, improve sleep quality, and boost the immune system.

How to Practice Mindful Meditation

Find a quiet place: Find a quiet and comfortable place where you can sit for at least 10-15 minutes without any distractions.

Sit comfortably: Sit in a comfortable position with your back straight, and your feet flat on the ground. You can sit on a cushion or a chair.

Close your eyes: Close your eyes and take a few deep breaths to help you relax.

Focus on your breath: Focus your attention on your breath, either at your nostrils or your abdomen. Notice the sensation of the air moving in and out of your body.

Observe your thoughts: As you focus on your breath, thoughts and feelings may arise. Observe them without judgment, and then gently bring your attention back to your breath.

Practice regularly: Practice mindful meditation for at least

08: MINDFUL MEDITATION: QUIETING THE MIND AND FINDING PEACE

10-15 minutes daily, preferably at the same time every day.

Tips for Incorporating Mindful Meditation into Your Daily Routine

Start small: If you're new to mindful meditation, start with just a few minutes a day and gradually increase the time.

Set a reminder: Set a reminder on your phone or calendar to remind you to practice mindful meditation at a specific time every day.

Be consistent: Consistency is key when it comes to mindful meditation. Make it a daily habit, just like brushing your teeth.

Use guided meditations: If you find it difficult to focus on your breath, use guided meditations that provide instructions and guidance.

Practice with others: Join a meditation group or attend a meditation retreat to deepen your practice and connect with like-minded individuals.

In Conclusion

08: MINDFUL MEDITATION: QUIETING THE MIND AND FINDING PEACE

Mindful meditation is a powerful tool that can help you quiet your mind, find inner peace, and transform your life. By incorporating mindful meditation into your daily routine, you can reduce stress and anxiety, improve emotional regulation, enhance focus and attention, boost creativity and innovation, and promote physical health. To practice mindful meditation, find a quiet place, sit comfortably, close your eyes, focus on your breath, observe your thoughts, and practice regularly. Start small, set a reminder, be consistent, use guided meditations, and practice with others to deepen your practice and connect with like-minded individuals.

Remember, the benefits of mindful meditation are not just limited to the time you spend meditating. The practice can help you cultivate a sense of mindfulness and presence in your daily life, allowing you to navigate challenging situations with greater ease and clarity. So take the time to incorporate mindful meditation into your daily routine, and experience the transformative power of quietness in your life.

09: Breathwork and Quietness: Harnessing the Power of Your Breath

Introduction

Breathwork is one of the most powerful tools we have to access quietness, reduce stress, and cultivate a sense of inner peace. It is a simple yet profound practice that can be done anywhere, anytime, and by anyone. In this chapter, we will explore the science behind breathwork, how it can help us manage stress and anxiety, and various techniques to incorporate breathwork into our daily lives.

The Science of Breathwork

Breathing is an involuntary process that we rarely pay attention to. However, when we consciously control our breathing, we can influence our physiological, emotional, and psychological state. Our breath is directly linked to our nervous system, and when we breathe deeply and rhythmically, we activate the parasympathetic nervous system, which is responsible for the relaxation response.

Breathwork has been found to have numerous health benefits, including lowering blood pressure, reducing anxiety and depression symptoms, increasing heart rate variability, improving immune function, and enhancing cognitive performance. Additionally, breathwork can improve our emotional regulation, self-awareness, and empathy.

The Practice of Breathwork

Breathwork can take many forms, including meditation, yoga, pranayama, and more. Below are some simple yet effective techniques to incorporate breathwork into your daily life.

Deep Breathing: Deep breathing is a simple yet powerful technique that can be done anywhere, anytime. Sit in a comfortable position with your back straight and your feet flat on the ground. Close your eyes and place one hand on your chest and the other hand on your belly. Inhale deeply through your nose, feeling your belly expand. Exhale slowly through your mouth, feeling your belly deflate. Repeat this for several minutes.

Box Breathing: Box breathing is a technique used by Navy SEALs to calm their nervous system before missions. Sit in a comfortable position and inhale deeply through your nose for four counts. Hold your breath for four counts. Exhale slowly through your mouth for four counts. Hold your breath for four counts. Repeat this for several minutes.

Alternate Nostril Breathing: Alternate nostril breathing is a yoga technique that can help balance the left and right hemispheres of the brain, calm the mind, and reduce stress. Sit in a comfortable position with your back straight. Use your right thumb to close your right nostril and inhale through your left nostril for four counts. Hold your breath for four counts. Use your right ring finger to close your left nostril and exhale through your right nostril for four counts. Inhale through your right nostril for four counts, hold your breath for four counts, then exhale through your left nostril for four counts. Repeat this for several minutes.

4-7-8 Breathing: 4-7-8 breathing is a technique developed by Dr. Andrew Weil that can help reduce anxiety and promote relaxation. Sit in a comfortable position with your back straight. Place the tip of your tongue behind your upper front teeth. Inhale deeply through your nose for four counts. Hold your breath for seven counts. Exhale slowly through your mouth, making a whooshing sound, for eight counts. Repeat this for several minutes.

Incorporating Breathwork into Your Daily Life

Breathwork can be incorporated into your daily life in various ways. You can start by setting aside a few minutes each day to practice deep breathing, box breathing, or another technique. You can also incorporate breathwork into your daily activities, such as while walking, exercising, or working. Whenever you feel stressed, anxious, or overwhelmed, take a few deep breaths and notice the difference in how you feel.

Conclusion

Breathwork is a powerful tool that can help us access quietness and cultivate inner peace. By understanding the science of breathwork and practicing various techniques, we can manage stress, reduce anxiety, and improve our overall health and wellbeing. The key to incorporating breathwork into our daily lives is to make it a habit and be consistent with our practice.

09: BREATHWORK AND QUIETNESS: HARNESSING THE POWER OF YOUR BREATH

As you continue to explore the power of breathwork, remember to be patient and gentle with yourself. Like any new habit, it may take time to see the full benefits of breathwork. However, with consistent practice, you will begin to notice a sense of calm and stillness within you that can transform your life.

In the next chapter, we will explore the importance of self-reflection and introspection in accessing quietness and finding inner peace. We will discuss the benefits of journaling, meditation, and other practices that can help us connect with our inner selves and unlock our full potential.

10: Finding Stillness in Nature: Connecting with the World Around You

As human beings, we are naturally drawn to the beauty of nature. From majestic mountains to rolling hills, tranquil lakes to roaring oceans, and vibrant forests to serene deserts, nature offers us a vast and diverse array of landscapes that captivate our senses and inspire our imagination. But beyond its aesthetic appeal, nature also has a profound impact on our emotional, mental, and spiritual well-being.

In a world that is increasingly fast-paced, noisy, and chaotic, finding stillness in nature can be a powerful way to reconnect with ourselves and cultivate inner peace. Whether we are walking through a park, sitting by a river, or gazing up at the stars, nature has a way of slowing us down and reminding us of the beauty and simplicity of life. In this chapter, we will explore the benefits of connecting with nature and offer some practical tips for incorporating nature into your daily life.

The Benefits of Connecting with Nature

10: FINDING STILLNESS IN NATURE: CONNECTING WITH THE WORLD AROUND YOU

Research has shown that spending time in nature can have a range of positive effects on our physical, emotional, and mental health. Here are just a few of the benefits of connecting with nature:

– Reduced stress and anxiety: Spending time in nature has been shown to reduce levels of the stress hormone cortisol and improve our mood and overall sense of well-being.

– Improved physical health: Being in nature can also have physical health benefits, such as reducing blood pressure, improving immune function, and increasing activity levels.

– Increased creativity: Nature has a way of inspiring us and sparking our creativity. Research has shown that exposure to nature can improve our problem-solving abilities and boost our creativity.

– Greater sense of connection: When we spend time in nature, we are reminded of our connection to the world around us. This can help us feel more grounded and connected to something larger than ourselves.

– Improved focus and attention: In a world that is full of

distractions, nature can help us focus our attention and improve our ability to concentrate.

Incorporating Nature into Your Daily Life

Now that we've explored some of the benefits of connecting with nature, let's look at some practical tips for incorporating nature into your daily life:

Take a walk in nature: Whether it's a local park, a nearby hiking trail, or a stroll around your neighborhood, taking a walk in nature can be a great way to clear your mind and reconnect with the world around you. Make it a daily habit to take a walk outside, even if it's just for a few minutes.

Bring nature indoors: Even if you can't get outside, bringing nature indoors can help you feel more connected to the natural world. Consider adding some plants to your home or workspace, or hanging nature-themed art on your walls.

Practice mindfulness in nature: When you're in nature, take the time to really be present and observe your surroundings. Use all of your senses to connect with the world around you, noticing the sights, sounds, smells, and textures of the natural world.

Take a digital detox: In a world that is increasingly connected, it can be hard to disconnect and find stillness. Consider taking a break from your phone, computer, and other digital devices and spending some time in nature instead.

Try a new outdoor activity: Whether it's kayaking, rock climbing, or birdwatching, trying a new outdoor activity can help you connect with nature in new and exciting ways.

Volunteer in a local park or conservation area: If you're passionate about protecting the environment, consider volunteering in a local park or conservation area. This can be a great way to connect with nature while also giving back to your community.

Practice gratitude for nature: Take the time to appreciate the beauty and wonder of the natural world. Practice gratitude for the gifts that nature provides, such as fresh air, clean water, and abundant food. When we feel grateful for something, we naturally become more mindful of it, and this can help us cultivate a deeper connection with nature.

10: FINDING STILLNESS IN NATURE: CONNECTING WITH THE WORLD AROUND YOU

Practice outdoor meditation: Find a quiet spot in nature and sit or lie down in a comfortable position. Close your eyes and focus on your breath, allowing your thoughts and emotions to come and go without judgment. Use nature as a focal point for your meditation, noticing the sensations of the sun, wind, or rain on your skin, the sounds of birds chirping or leaves rustling, and the scents of flowers or trees.

Take a nature retreat: Consider taking a few days to disconnect from your daily routine and immerse yourself in nature. Whether it's a camping trip, a cabin rental, or a yoga retreat, spending time in nature can be a powerful way to recharge your batteries and gain a fresh perspective on life.

Create a nature journal: Keep a journal of your experiences in nature, including your thoughts, feelings, and observations. This can be a great way to reflect on your connection with the natural world and track your progress over time.

In conclusion, finding stillness in nature can be a powerful way to connect with ourselves, cultivate inner peace, and transform our lives. By incorporating nature into our daily routines and taking the time to appreciate its beauty and wonder, we can tap into a deep well of wisdom, creativity, and joy that can help us navigate the challenges of life with greater ease and grace. So the next time you're feeling stressed, overwhelmed, or disconnected, take a deep breath and step outside. The natural world is waiting to welcome you with open arms.

11: The Power of Sound: Finding Quietness in Noise

As humans, we are constantly surrounded by sound. From the bustling city streets to the chirping of birds, our ears are always picking up some kind of noise. While some sounds can be pleasant and soothing, others can be overwhelming and stressful.

Noise pollution has become a significant issue in our society today, with loud traffic, construction sites, and other sources of noise disrupting the tranquility of our everyday lives. The constant noise can lead to a sense of unease, making it difficult to concentrate, relax, or even sleep.

However, it is possible to find quietness amidst the noise. The power of sound can be harnessed to help us achieve a sense of inner peace and tranquility. In this chapter, we will explore how sound can be used to unlock the power of quietness and find inner peace.

Understanding Sound

Sound is a physical phenomenon that is created by the vibration of particles in the air. When an object vibrates, it causes the air particles around it to vibrate as well, creating sound waves that travel through the air. These sound waves then enter our ears, where they are transformed into electrical signals that are sent to our brain, allowing us to perceive the sound.

Sound has a significant impact on our mental and emotional well-being. Certain sounds can evoke feelings of joy, relaxation, and contentment, while others can cause anxiety, stress, and discomfort. For example, the sound of rain can be soothing and calming, while the sound of a car alarm can be irritating and stressful.

Sound and the Brain

Our brain plays a crucial role in how we perceive and react to sound. The auditory cortex, located in the temporal lobe of the brain, is responsible for processing sound. It receives signals from the ears and interprets them as sound, allowing us to identify and understand what we are hearing.

Sound also has the power to affect our brain waves. Different types of sound can influence our brain waves, which can impact our mental and emotional state. For example, listening to soothing music can slow down our brain waves, leading to a sense of calmness and relaxation.

Finding Quietness in Noise

While it may seem impossible to find quietness amidst the noise, it is possible with the right mindset and approach. Here are some strategies for finding quietness in noise:

Mindful Listening: Instead of trying to block out the noise, try to listen to it mindfully. Focus on the different sounds you can hear and try to identify each one. This can help you become more aware of your surroundings and appreciate the beauty of sound.

White Noise: White noise refers to a type of sound that contains all frequencies of sound at equal levels. It can be used to mask other sounds and create a sense of calmness. White noise machines are widely available and can be used to create a peaceful environment for sleeping or working.

Music: Listening to calming music can help you relax and reduce stress. There are many types of music that can be used for relaxation, including classical, ambient, and nature sounds. Experiment with different types of music to find what works best for you.

Nature Sounds: The sound of nature, such as the chirping of birds or the sound of waves crashing on the shore, can be incredibly calming and soothing. Listening to nature sounds can help you feel more connected to the natural world and reduce stress.

Silence: Sometimes, the best way to find quietness is by embracing silence. Turn off all electronics and sit in silence for a few minutes each day. This can help you clear your mind and find a sense of inner peace.

Conclusion

Sound is a powerful tool that can be used to unlock the power of quietness and find inner peace. By understanding how sound works and how it affects our brain and emotions, we can learn to use sound to our advantage and create a more peaceful environment for ourselves. Mindful listening, white noise, music, nature sounds, and silence are all effective strategies for finding quietness in noise.

11: THE POWER OF SOUND: FINDING QUIETNESS IN NOISE

Incorporating these strategies into your daily routine can help you reduce stress, improve focus, and increase your overall sense of well-being. It's important to remember that everyone is different, and what works for one person may not work for another. Experiment with different strategies and find what works best for you.

It's also important to note that while sound can be used to create a sense of calmness and tranquility, it's not a substitute for dealing with underlying issues. If you're experiencing chronic stress or anxiety, it's important to seek professional help and address the root cause of the issue.

In summary, the power of sound can be harnessed to help us find quietness in noise and achieve a sense of inner peace. By becoming more mindful of the sounds around us and incorporating strategies such as white noise, music, and nature sounds into our daily routine, we can create a more peaceful environment for ourselves and improve our mental and emotional well-being.

12: The Quietness of Creativity: Finding Inspiration in Solitude

In today's fast-paced world, it's easy to feel like we're constantly on the go. Our schedules are packed with meetings, appointments, and social events, leaving little time for quiet reflection and introspection. We're bombarded with information and stimulation from all sides, and it can be hard to find a moment of peace and stillness in the midst of all the chaos.

But what if I told you that the key to unlocking your creativity and finding inspiration is to embrace the power of quietness? What if I told you that the most innovative and creative minds throughout history have often found their greatest insights and breakthroughs in moments of solitude and stillness?

In this chapter, we'll explore the connection between quietness and creativity, and offer some practical tips and strategies for finding inspiration in solitude.

The Power of Solitude

Let's start by acknowledging that solitude can be a scary

prospect for many people. We're social creatures, and the idea of being alone with our thoughts can be intimidating. But solitude doesn't have to mean loneliness or isolation. Instead, think of it as an opportunity to tune out external distractions and focus on your inner world.

When we're constantly surrounded by noise and stimulation, our minds become cluttered and overloaded. We struggle to concentrate and find it hard to come up with new ideas or perspectives. But when we take a step back and allow ourselves to experience the quietness of solitude, we give our brains a chance to rest and reset.

In fact, research has shown that moments of solitude can be incredibly beneficial for our mental health and well-being. Studies have found that people who regularly take time to be alone with their thoughts are better able to regulate their emotions, process difficult experiences, and maintain a sense of inner calm and resilience.

So if you're feeling stuck or uninspired in your creative pursuits, consider setting aside some time to be alone with your thoughts. Whether it's a few minutes of quiet reflection each day, a weekend retreat in nature, or a solo trip to a new city, there are many ways to embrace the power of solitude and find inspiration in the quietness.

The Creative Benefits of Stillness

But why does solitude and quietness help us tap into our creativity? The answer lies in the way our brains function. When we're constantly bombarded with information and stimulation, our brains become overloaded and struggle to process new information effectively. But when we give ourselves a break from external distractions and allow our minds to wander, we create space for new connections and insights to emerge.

This is why many artists, writers, and other creative thinkers throughout history have found their greatest ideas and breakthroughs in moments of stillness and quietness. Think of Henry David Thoreau, who spent two years living alone in a cabin in the woods and wrote his masterpiece, "Walden," during that time. Or composer Ludwig van Beethoven, who would often take long walks in the countryside to clear his mind and find inspiration for his music.

Even in our modern era, many successful entrepreneurs

and business leaders have embraced the power of stillness and quietness as a key component of their creative process. For example, Steve Jobs was known for his regular meditation practice, which he credited with helping him stay focused and generate new ideas.

Practical Strategies for Finding Inspiration in Solitude

So how can you incorporate the power of quietness into your own creative process? Here are a few practical strategies to try:

Make time for daily reflection. Whether it's a few minutes of meditation or journaling each morning, or a quiet walk in the park during your lunch break, try to carve out a few moments each day to be alone with your thoughts and reflect on your goals and aspirations.

Take a solo retreat. Consider taking a weekend or longer to retreat from the noise and distractions of your everyday life and immerse yourself in a new environment that inspires you. This could be a cabin in the woods, a beachside cottage, or a remote mountain retreat. Use this time to reflect, recharge, and tap into your creative potential.

12: THE QUIETNESS OF CREATIVITY: FINDING INSPIR-ATION IN SOLITUDE

Practice mindfulness. Mindfulness meditation is a powerful tool for cultivating inner stillness and focus. By training your mind to stay present in the moment, you can develop greater clarity, creativity, and resilience.

Engage in creative hobbies. Whether it's painting, writing, or playing an instrument, creative hobbies can be a great way to tap into your inner creativity and find inspiration in the quietness of solitude. Make time to pursue activities that bring you joy and allow you to express yourself creatively.

Disconnect from technology. In our hyperconnected world, it's easy to become overwhelmed by the constant stream of information and stimulation. Consider taking a break from social media, email, and other digital distractions, and give yourself time to disconnect and recharge.

The Quietness of Creativity: Final Thoughts

In the end, the key to unlocking your creativity and finding inspiration lies in embracing the power of quietness. Whether you're a writer, artist, entrepreneur, or simply someone looking to tap into your inner potential, taking time to be alone with your thoughts and embrace stillness can help you cultivate greater clarity, focus, and creativity.

So don't be afraid to step away from the noise and distractions of everyday life and immerse yourself in the quietness
of solitude. Use this time to reflect, recharge, and tap into
your inner potential. Who knows what new ideas and insights you might discover?

13: The Role of Technology in Quietness

In today's world, technology has become an essential part of our lives. It has made our lives more comfortable, efficient, and convenient, but it has also made it more challenging to find moments of quietness and solitude. The constant barrage of notifications, emails, texts, and social media updates can create a sense of anxiety and distract us from the present moment. In this chapter, we will explore the role of technology in quietness and how we can use it to our advantage.

The Impact of Technology on Quietness

The rise of technology has had a significant impact on our ability to find moments of quietness in our lives. The constant availability of smartphones, laptops, and other digital devices means that we are always connected to the world, even when we should be taking time to disconnect and recharge. The constant stimulation of technology can make it challenging to focus on the present moment, and it can also lead to increased levels of stress and anxiety.

Studies have shown that the overuse of technology can have

a negative impact on our mental health. It can lead to symptoms of depression, anxiety, and addiction. The constant stimulation of technology can also lead to sleep disturbances and a lack of concentration, making it challenging to find moments of quietness and focus on the present moment.

However, technology can also be a tool that we can use to our advantage to find moments of quietness and solitude. There are many apps and tools available that can help us manage our technology use and find moments of quietness in our lives.

Using Technology to Find Quietness

Technology can be a double-edged sword when it comes to finding moments of quietness. On the one hand, it can be a distraction that pulls us away from the present moment. On the other hand, it can be a tool that helps us manage our time and create opportunities for quietness and solitude.

Here are some ways that we can use technology to find moments of quietness in our lives:

Meditation Apps

Meditation apps are a popular way to find moments of quietness and focus on the present moment. There are many meditation apps available that offer guided meditations, mindfulness exercises, and relaxation techniques. These apps can be a helpful tool for managing stress and anxiety and finding moments of quietness in our lives.

Digital Detox Apps

Digital detox apps are designed to help us manage our technology use and find moments of quietness in our lives. These apps can track our phone usage, set limits on our screen time, and offer reminders to take breaks from technology. Digital detox apps can be a helpful tool for managing our technology use and finding moments of quietness in our lives.

Mindfulness Apps

Mindfulness apps are designed to help us focus on the present moment and find moments of quietness in our lives. These apps offer mindfulness exercises, breathing techniques, and other tools to help us manage stress and anxiety and find moments of quietness in our lives.

13: THE ROLE OF TECHNOLOGY IN QUIETNESS

Nature Apps

Nature apps are designed to help us connect with nature and find moments of quietness in our lives. These apps offer virtual tours of nature, nature sounds, and other tools to help us relax and find moments of quietness in our lives.

Productivity Apps

Productivity apps are designed to help us manage our time and increase our productivity. By managing our time more effectively, we can create opportunities for quietness and solitude in our lives. Productivity apps can be a helpful tool for finding moments of quietness in our lives.

The Bottom Line

Technology has become an integral part of our lives, but it can also be a source of stress and anxiety. By using technology to our advantage, we can find moments of quietness and solitude in our lives. Meditation apps, digital detox apps, mindfulness apps, nature apps, and productivity apps are just a few examples of how we can use technology to find moments of quietness in our lives. However, it's important to remember that technology should be used as a tool to help us find quietness, not as a substitute for it.

It's also important to be mindful of our technology use and take breaks from it when necessary. This can help us avoid becoming overwhelmed and stressed by the constant stimulation of technology.

In addition to using technology, there are other ways to find moments of quietness in our lives. These can include spending time in nature, practicing yoga or meditation, reading a book, or simply taking a walk.

Ultimately, the key to finding moments of quietness in our lives is to be intentional about it. We need to make it a priority and actively seek out opportunities for quietness and solitude. By doing so, we can reduce our stress and anxiety, improve our mental health, and find lasting happiness and fulfillment.

Conclusion

In conclusion, technology has had a significant impact on our ability to find moments of quietness and solitude in our lives. While it can be a source of stress and distraction, it can also be a tool that we can use to our advantage.

13: THE ROLE OF TECHNOLOGY IN QUIETNESS

By using apps and other tools designed to help us manage our technology use and find moments of quietness, we can reduce our stress and anxiety and improve our overall well-being. However, it's important to remember that technology should be used as a tool to help us find quietness, not as a substitute for it.

Ultimately, finding moments of quietness and solitude in our lives requires intentionality and effort. By making it a priority and actively seeking out opportunities for quietness and solitude, we can improve our mental health, reduce our stress, and find lasting happiness and fulfillment.

14: Mindfulness in Everyday Life: Bringing Quietness into Your Daily Routine

Quietness is a powerful force that can transform our lives, but it's not always easy to find in the midst of our busy, hectic routines. We live in a world that values constant activity and stimulation, and it can be hard to slow down and cultivate inner peace. But mindfulness can help us bring the power of quietness into our everyday lives.

Mindfulness is the practice of being fully present and aware in the present moment, without judgment or distraction. It's a way of tuning in to our thoughts, emotions, and physical sensations with a sense of curiosity and openness. And it can be practiced in any moment, whether we're washing the dishes, walking to work, or sitting in meditation.

One of the keys to mindfulness is learning to cultivate a non-judgmental attitude towards our thoughts and feelings. Often, we have a tendency to judge ourselves harshly for our perceived shortcomings or mistakes, or to get caught up in negative thought patterns that only exacerbate our stress and anxiety. But by learning to observe our thoughts and emotions without judgment, we can begin to see them more objectively and learn to let go of unhelpful patterns.

Another important aspect of mindfulness is cultivating an attitude of kindness and compassion towards ourselves and others. It's easy to get caught up in a cycle of self-criticism and judgment, but this only serves to reinforce negative beliefs about ourselves and limit our potential for growth. By cultivating a sense of self-compassion, we can learn to treat ourselves with kindness and understanding, even when we make mistakes or encounter difficulties.

So how can we bring mindfulness into our everyday lives? Here are a few tips and strategies:

Start small. You don't have to set aside hours of your day for meditation or mindfulness practice. Instead, try starting with just a few minutes each day. Set a timer for five or ten minutes, and simply focus on your breath or a particular sensation in your body. As you become more comfortable with this practice, you can gradually increase the amount of time you spend in mindfulness.

Practice mindfulness in everyday activities. You don't have

to be sitting on a meditation cushion to practice mindfulness. You can bring this awareness into any activity, whether it's walking, washing the dishes, or even brushing your teeth. Simply focus your attention on the present moment, and allow yourself to fully experience whatever you're doing.

Use mindfulness as a tool for stress relief. When we're feeling stressed or anxious, it can be helpful to take a few moments to tune in to our breath or physical sensations. By focusing on the present moment, we can calm our nervous system and reduce feelings of anxiety or overwhelm.

Incorporate mindfulness into your daily routine. One way to make mindfulness a habit is to incorporate it into your daily routine. For example, you might set an intention to be mindful while you're waiting in line at the grocery store, or to take a few deep breaths before you start your workday.

Find a mindfulness community. Practicing mindfulness can be a solitary activity, but it can also be helpful to connect with others who are on the same journey. Consider joining a mindfulness group or attending a meditation class to deepen your practice and connect with like-minded individuals.

As you begin to incorporate mindfulness into your daily routine, you may notice a shift in your perspective and your experience of the world around you. By tuning in to the present moment, you can cultivate a sense of peace and quietness that can help you navigate even the most challenging circumstances. So take a deep breath, and allow yourself to fully embrace the power of mindfulness in your everyday life.

15: Spiritual Quietness: Nurturing Your Inner Life

In a world that is constantly moving, it is easy to feel overwhelmed, anxious, and stressed. From the moment we wake up, we are bombarded with notifications, messages, and reminders of everything we need to do. It is no wonder that many of us feel a deep longing for quietness, for a chance to disconnect from the noise and find peace in the stillness.

But what is quietness, really? Is it just the absence of noise, or is it something more? Spiritual quietness is about nurturing your inner life, connecting with your deepest self, and finding meaning and purpose in your existence. It is about discovering the beauty and wisdom that lie within you, and learning to live in alignment with your true nature.

The path to spiritual quietness is not an easy one, but it is a rewarding one. It requires courage, patience, and a willingness to face your fears, doubts, and limitations. But if you are willing to take that journey, you will discover a treasure trove of insights, strategies, and practices that will help you transform your life and find lasting happiness.

Here are some of the key principles and practices of spir-

15: SPIRITUAL QUIETNESS: NURTURING YOUR INNER LIFE

itual quietness:

Embrace solitude

Solitude is not the same as loneliness. Loneliness is a feeling of disconnection and isolation, while solitude is a choice to be alone with your thoughts and feelings. It is a precious opportunity to reflect, recharge, and connect with your inner wisdom. When you embrace solitude, you give yourself permission to be still, to listen to your heart, and to let your intuition guide you.

Cultivate mindfulness

Mindfulness is the art of paying attention to the present moment, without judgment or distraction. When you cultivate mindfulness, you learn to observe your thoughts, feelings, and sensations with curiosity and compassion. You become more aware of your patterns, habits, and triggers, and you gain the power to choose how you respond to them.

Practice gratitude

Gratitude is the practice of focusing on the good things in your life, and acknowledging the blessings that you have received. When you practice gratitude, you shift your perspective from lack to abundance, from negativity to positivity. You become more aware of the beauty and wonder that surrounds you, and you develop a sense of awe and reverence for life.

Connect with nature

Nature is a powerful source of inspiration, healing, and renewal. When you connect with nature, you tap into the rhythms and cycles of life, and you become more attuned to the natural world. You may find solace in the sound of the wind, the rustle of leaves, or the song of birds. You may find clarity in the vastness of the sky, the depth of the ocean, or the majesty of mountains. You may find peace in the simplicity of a flower, the symmetry of a butterfly, or the grace of a deer.

Explore your creativity

Creativity is the expression of your unique voice, vision, and talent. When you explore your creativity, you tap into the infinite possibilities of your imagination, and you give yourself permission to play, experiment, and innovate. You may find joy in the process of painting, writing, singing, dancing, or any other form of self-expression. You may find fulfillment in the sense of accomplishment, the feedback of others, or the impact of your work.

Practice self-care

Self-care is the practice of taking care of your physical, mental, and emotional health. When you practice self-care, you honor your needs, boundaries, and values, and you prioritize your well-being. You may find comfort in the routine of exercise, sleep, nutrition, and hygiene. You may find support in the company of friends, family, or professionals. You may find growth in the challenges of therapy , meditation, or other self-reflection practices.

Cultivate compassion

Compassion is the practice of empathy, kindness, and understanding towards yourself and others. When you cultivate compassion, you learn to forgive yourself for your mistakes, and to see the humanity in others despite their flaws. You may find healing in the act of forgiveness, the sense of connection, and the opportunity for growth.

15: SPIRITUAL QUIETNESS: NURTURING YOUR INNER LIFE

Seek wisdom

Wisdom is the insight, knowledge, and understanding that comes from experience, reflection, and learning. When you seek wisdom, you open yourself to the vastness of human knowledge and experience, and you become more aware of your own limitations and biases. You may find guidance in the teachings of spiritual traditions, the writings of philosophers and thinkers, or the stories and experiences of those who came before you.

Live with intention

Living with intention means setting clear goals, values, and priorities for your life, and aligning your actions and choices with them. When you live with intention, you become more focused, purposeful, and disciplined, and you avoid the distractions and temptations that can pull you off course. You may find fulfillment in the sense of purpose, the achievement of your goals, and the impact of your actions.

Trust the journey

Finally, spiritual quietness is about trusting the journey,

even when it is uncertain, difficult, or painful. When you trust the journey, you acknowledge that life is full of ups and downs, and that growth and transformation often come from the challenges and setbacks we face. You may find courage in the face of adversity, the resilience to bounce back from setbacks, and the faith that everything happens for a reason.

In conclusion, spiritual quietness is a powerful path to self-discovery, personal growth, and lasting happiness. By embracing solitude, cultivating mindfulness, practicing gratitude, connecting with nature, exploring your creativity, practicing self-care, cultivating compassion, seeking wisdom, living with intention, and trusting the journey, you can unlock the power of quietness and transform your life in profound ways.

16: The Journey Inward: Self-Discovery Through Quietness

The journey inward is a transformative process of self-discovery that leads to personal growth and lasting happiness. It is a journey that requires one to embrace quietness and solitude, to turn away from the distractions and noise of the external world, and to delve deep into the inner self.

In today's fast-paced and noisy world, it is easy to get caught up in the endless stream of external stimuli. We are bombarded with information, entertainment, and stimulation from the moment we wake up to the moment we go to bed. We have become so accustomed to the noise that we often forget to pause and listen to the quietness within us. We forget that the real journey of self-discovery begins when we start listening to ourselves.

The journey inward is not an easy one. It requires a great deal of courage, patience, and self-awareness. It is a journey that can be challenging, but it is also a journey that is incredibly rewarding. When we embark on the journey inward, we begin to discover the true essence of who we are. We begin to understand our fears, our desires, our passions, and our purpose in life.

16: THE JOURNEY INWARD: SELF-DISCOVERY THROUGH QUIETNESS

To embark on the journey inward, we must first learn to embrace quietness and solitude. We must learn to turn off the noise of the external world and tune in to the quietness within us. This can be achieved through meditation, mindfulness, or simply taking a quiet walk in nature. Whatever method we choose, the goal is to create a space within ourselves where we can hear our own thoughts and feelings.

As we learn to embrace quietness and solitude, we begin to develop a deeper sense of self-awareness. We begin to understand our own patterns of behavior, our strengths and weaknesses, and our core values. This self-awareness is essential for personal growth, as it allows us to identify areas in our lives where we want to make changes.

The journey inward also requires us to confront our fears and our past. We must be willing to face the parts of ourselves that we may not want to see. We must be willing to examine our beliefs and values and question whether they are serving us well. This can be a painful process, but it is also a necessary one if we want to grow and evolve.

As we continue on the journey inward, we begin to discover our passions and our purpose in life. We begin to understand what makes us happy and what brings us meaning. This self-discovery allows us to align our actions with our values and to create a life that is fulfilling and satisfying.

The journey inward is not a one-time event. It is an ongoing process of self-discovery and personal growth. As we continue to grow and evolve, we will encounter new challenges and opportunities for growth. We must remain committed to the journey inward and continue to embrace quietness and solitude as a way to connect with our inner selves.

In conclusion, the journey inward is a transformative process of self-discovery that leads to personal growth and lasting happiness. It requires us to embrace quietness and solitude, to turn away from the distractions and noise of the external world, and to delve deep into the inner self. It is a journey that can be challenging, but it is also a journey that is incredibly rewarding. Through the journey inward, we can discover our passions, our purpose, and our true selves.

17: The Power of Gratitude: Finding Peace in the Present Moment

The power of gratitude is an often-overlooked aspect of our daily lives. Yet, it is one of the most powerful tools we have at our disposal to transform our lives and find inner peace. Gratitude helps us to focus on the present moment, to appreciate the little things, and to find joy in the everyday. In this chapter, we will explore the benefits of practicing gratitude, and we will provide you with the tools and strategies you need to cultivate a grateful mindset and transform your life.

Gratitude is a state of mind that involves acknowledging and appreciating the good things in our lives. It is the act of recognizing and expressing appreciation for the people, experiences, and things that make our lives better. When we practice gratitude, we shift our focus away from what we lack and onto what we have, which can have a profound impact on our overall well-being.

Research has shown that practicing gratitude can have numerous benefits for our mental and physical health. It has been linked to increased happiness, reduced stress and anxiety, improved sleep, and even a stronger immune system. When we focus on the positive aspects of our lives, we are better able to cope with challenges and setbacks, and we are more likely to experience a sense of peace and contentment.

So, how can we cultivate a grateful mindset? There are several strategies and techniques that can help us to practice gratitude on a daily basis.

Keep a gratitude journal

One of the most effective ways to cultivate a grateful mindset is to keep a gratitude journal. Each day, take a few minutes to write down three to five things that you are grateful for. They can be big or small, significant or insignificant. The point is to focus on the positive aspects of your life and to appreciate the good things that you have. Over time, this practice can help to retrain your brain to focus on the positive aspects of your life, and to cultivate a more optimistic outlook.

Practice mindfulness

Mindfulness is the practice of being fully present in the moment, without judgment or distraction. When we practice mindfulness, we are better able to appreciate the little things in life and to find joy in the present moment. One way to practice mindfulness is to focus on your senses. Take a few minutes to notice the sights, sounds, smells, and sensations around you. Notice the way the sunlight filters through the leaves, the sound of birds chirping, the scent of fresh coffee, or the feel of the breeze on your skin. By focusing on the present moment and appreciating the sensory experiences around us, we can cultivate a greater sense of gratitude and inner peace.

Express gratitude to others

Expressing gratitude to others is a powerful way to cultivate a grateful mindset. Take a few moments each day to express gratitude to the people in your life who make a difference. It can be as simple as thanking a coworker for their help on a project, complimenting a friend on their outfit, or telling your partner how much you appreciate their love and support. By expressing gratitude to others, we not only cultivate a greater sense of gratitude within ourselves, but we also strengthen our relationships and build a more positive and supportive community.

Practice gratitude in difficult situations

Practicing gratitude in difficult situations can be a challenge, but it is also one of the most powerful ways to transform our mindset and find peace in the present moment. When we face challenges or setbacks, it can be easy to focus on the negative aspects of the situation. However, by practicing gratitude, we can shift our focus away from what we lack and onto what we have. For example, if you are struggling with a difficult project at work, you can focus on the skills and resources you have that can help you overcome the challenge. If you are dealing with a health issue, you can to focus on the positive aspects of your life, such as your relationships, your hobbies, or your personal strengths. By reframing our thoughts in a more positive light, we can find strength and resilience in the face of adversity.

Create a gratitude ritual

Creating a gratitude ritual is a powerful way to incorporate gratitude into your daily life. This could be as simple as taking a few moments each morning to reflect on what you are grateful for, or as elaborate as creating a gratitude altar or ritual space in your home. The point is to create a consistent practice that reminds you to focus on the positive aspects of your life and to cultivate a grateful mindset.

Incorporating these strategies into your daily life can help you to cultivate a grateful mindset and transform your life. However, it's important to remember that cultivating gratitude is a practice, and it takes time and effort to develop a more positive outlook. Don't be discouraged if you don't see results immediately. Keep practicing, and over time, you will begin to notice a profound shift in your mindset and your overall well-being.

In addition to these practical strategies, there are also several deeper insights and perspectives that can help us to cultivate a more grateful mindset.

Firstly, it's important to recognize that gratitude is not about denying or minimizing the challenges and struggles that we face in life. Rather, it's about finding the good in the midst of the difficulties. By acknowledging the challenges and choosing to focus on the positive aspects of our lives, we can find greater strength and resilience to face whatever comes our way.

Secondly, it's important to recognize that gratitude is not about comparing ourselves to others. It's not about measuring our blessings against someone else's, or feeling guilty for what we have when others have less. Gratitude is about recognizing and appreciating the good in our own lives, without judgment or comparison.

Finally, it's important to recognize that gratitude is not about being happy all the time. Life is full of ups and downs, and we will inevitably experience difficult times. However, by cultivating a grateful mindset, we can find moments of joy and peace even in the midst of the challenges.

In conclusion, the power of gratitude is a profound and transformative force in our lives. By cultivating a grateful mindset, we can find inner peace, joy, and contentment, even in the midst of the challenges and difficulties of life. Whether through practical strategies or deeper insights and perspectives, the power of gratitude is available to all of us, and it has the potential to transform our lives in ways we never imagined. So, take a moment right now to reflect on what you are grateful for, and let that gratitude fill your heart and transform your life.

18: Overcoming Anxiety with Quietness

Anxiety is one of the most prevalent mental health conditions in the world today. It can affect anyone at any time, regardless of age, gender, or race. Anxiety can manifest itself in different ways, from mild to severe, and can disrupt a person's daily activities and relationships. While there are different approaches to managing anxiety, embracing quietness can be a powerful tool in overcoming this condition.

In this chapter, we will explore how quietness can help you overcome anxiety. We will discuss the causes of anxiety, the symptoms of anxiety, and the proven strategies and insights of quietness that can help you find inner peace, manage your emotions, and transform your life.

Causes of Anxiety

Anxiety can be caused by a variety of factors, including genetics, environment, life experiences, and other medical conditions. For some people, anxiety may be triggered by a traumatic event, such as abuse or the loss of a loved one. For others, it may be a result of ongoing stress or chronic health conditions.

Anxiety can also be a symptom of other mental health conditions, such as depression or bipolar disorder. In some cases, anxiety may be a side effect of medication or substance abuse.

Symptoms of Anxiety

The symptoms of anxiety can vary from person to person, but some common symptoms include:

– Restlessness or feeling on edge

– Difficulty concentrating

– Irritability

– Muscle tension

– Sleep disturbances

– Panic attacks

– Avoidance of social situations

– Excessive worry

These symptoms can interfere with a person's daily activities and relationships, leading to feelings of frustration, helplessness, and hopelessness. Fortunately, there are strategies and insights that can help you manage anxiety and find inner peace.

Proven Strategies and Insights of Quietness

Quietness is a state of being calm, still, and at peace with oneself and one's surroundings. It is a powerful tool for managing anxiety, as it can help you quiet your mind, focus on the present moment, and find inner peace. Here are some proven strategies and insights of quietness that can help you overcome anxiety:

Mindfulness Meditation

Mindfulness meditation is a technique that involves focusing your attention on the present moment, without judgment. It can help you quiet your mind, reduce stress, and improve your overall well-being. To practice mindfulness meditation, find a quiet place to sit comfortably, close your eyes, and focus on your breath. If your mind wanders, gently bring your attention back to your breath.

Deep Breathing

Deep breathing is a simple but effective technique for reducing anxiety. It can help you slow down your breathing, lower your heart rate, and calm your mind. To practice deep breathing, find a quiet place to sit or lie down, and breathe in slowly through your nose for a count of four. Hold your breath for a count of four, then exhale slowly through your mouth for a count of four. Repeat this cycle for several minutes.

Visualization

Visualization is a technique that involves imagining a peaceful scene or situation. It can help you relax and reduce anxiety by distracting your mind from negative thoughts. To practice visualization, find a quiet place to sit or lie down, close your eyes, and imagine a peaceful scene, such as a beach or a forest. Visualize the scene in detail, using all your senses, and focus on the sensations of peace and relaxation.

Gratitude

Gratitude is a powerful tool for reducing anxiety and improving your overall well-being. It can help you shift your focus from negative thoughts to positive ones, and increase feelings of happiness and contentment. To practice gratitude, make a list of things you are grateful for, such as your health, your family, or your job. Take a few minutes each day to reflect on your list and express your gratitude for these things.

Self-Care

Self-care is an essential part of managing anxiety. It involves taking care of your physical, emotional, and mental well-being. Some self-care practices include exercise, healthy eating, getting enough sleep, and engaging in activities that bring you joy and relaxation. It is essential to prioritize self-care in your daily routine to maintain a healthy balance and reduce stress and anxiety.

Mindful Breathing

Mindful breathing is another technique that can help you reduce anxiety and find inner peace. It involves paying attention to your breath and observing it without judgment. To practice mindful breathing, find a quiet place to sit or lie down, close your eyes, and focus on your breath. Observe the sensations of your breath, such as the rising and falling of your chest, and the temperature of the air as it enters and exits your body.

18: OVERCOMING ANXIETY WITH QUIETNESS

Acceptance

Acceptance is a key component of managing anxiety. It involves acknowledging and accepting your thoughts and feelings, without trying to change them. Instead of fighting against your anxiety, try to accept it and observe it without judgment. This can help you reduce the intensity of your anxiety and find inner peace.

Journaling

Journaling is an effective tool for managing anxiety. It involves writing down your thoughts and feelings, which can help you process and understand them better. To journal, find a quiet place to sit down and write about your thoughts and feelings. You can also use journaling to practice gratitude, set goals, and reflect on your personal growth.

Nature

Spending time in nature can be a powerful tool for managing anxiety. It can help you reduce stress, find inner peace, and connect with the natural world. Try to spend some time in nature each day, whether it's taking a walk in a park, sitting in a garden, or simply observing the sky.

18: OVERCOMING ANXIETY WITH QUIETNESS

Mindful Eating

Mindful eating is a technique that involves paying attention to your food and eating it slowly and intentionally. It can help you reduce stress and anxiety, improve digestion, and increase feelings of satisfaction and well-being. To practice mindful eating, take your time to chew your food, savor its flavors, and pay attention to your body's signals of hunger and fullness.

In conclusion, anxiety can be a challenging condition to manage, but embracing quietness can be a powerful tool in overcoming it. By practicing mindfulness meditation, deep breathing, visualization, gratitude, self-care, mindful breathing, acceptance, journaling, spending time in nature, and mindful eating, you can reduce anxiety, find inner peace, and transform your life. Remember to prioritize self-care and seek professional help if you need it. With time and practice, you can overcome anxiety and embrace the power of quietness in your life.

19: Quietness and Emotional Intelligence: Deepening Your Self-Awareness

In today's fast-paced world, quietness seems to be a lost art. We are always on the go, constantly bombarded by noise and distractions, and have become accustomed to a culture of busyness. We measure our success by how busy we are, how many tasks we complete, and how many people we can multitask with at the same time. But what if I told you that the secret to self-discovery, personal growth, and lasting happiness lies in the power of quietness?

The benefits of quietness are well-known, yet often overlooked. Quietness allows us to slow down, reflect, and cultivate our inner wisdom. It helps us to better understand ourselves, our thoughts, and our emotions. Quietness also allows us to recharge our energy, reduce stress, and enhance our overall well-being.

But the real magic of quietness lies in its ability to deepen our emotional intelligence. Emotional intelligence is the ability to recognize, understand, and manage our own emotions, as well as those of others. It's a critical skill that plays a key role in our personal and professional lives, and in our overall happiness.

So, how can quietness help us to develop our emotional intelligence? Let's explore some proven strategies and insights.

Practice mindfulness

Mindfulness is the practice of being present and fully engaged in the present moment, without judgment. It's a powerful tool that helps us to become more self-aware, and to tune into our thoughts, feelings, and physical sensations.

One way to practice mindfulness is through meditation. Find a quiet space, sit comfortably, and focus your attention on your breath. Notice the sensations of the breath as it enters and leaves your body. When your mind wanders, gently bring it back to your breath. You can start with just a few minutes a day and gradually increase the time.

Journaling

Journaling is a powerful tool for self-reflection and self-discovery. It allows us to explore our thoughts, feelings, and emotions in a safe and non-judgmental way. It's a way to release our innermost thoughts and emotions, and to gain clarity and insight into our lives.

Take a few minutes each day to write down your thoughts, feelings, and emotions. You can also use journaling as a tool for self-reflection by asking yourself questions such as "What am I grateful for today?" or "What did I learn from this experience?"

Take time for solitude

Solitude is the state of being alone, without distractions. It's a time to disconnect from the outside world and to tune into our inner world. Solitude allows us to reflect, recharge, and gain perspective.

Make time for solitude each day, even if it's just a few minutes. Turn off your phone, computer, and other distractions, and simply be with yourself. You can use this time to meditate, journal, or simply sit quietly and reflect.

Listen to your emotions

Our emotions are powerful signals that give us information

about our inner world. They tell us when something is wrong, when we need to make a change, or when we are on the right track. But often, we ignore our emotions or try to suppress them.

Instead, try to listen to your emotions and use them as a guide. When you feel a strong emotion, take a moment to tune into it. Ask yourself what it's trying to tell you, and what action you need to take.

Practice empathy

Empathy is the ability to understand and feel the emotions of others. It's a critical skill that allows us to connect with others on a deeper level, and to build strong relationships.

Practice empathy by actively listening to others, putting yourself in their shoes, and trying to understand their perspective. When you encounter someone who is struggling with their emotions, offer them a listening ear and show compassion. By practicing empathy, you'll not only strengthen your emotional intelligence but also cultivate stronger relationships with others.

19: QUIETNESS AND EMOTIONAL INTELLIGENCE: DEEPENING YOUR SELF-AWARENESS

Cultivate self-compassion

Self-compassion is the practice of treating ourselves with kindness, care, and understanding. It's about recognizing that we are human and imperfect, and that we all make mistakes. Self-compassion allows us to be kind to ourselves, even when we're struggling.

Practice self-compassion by treating yourself with the same kindness and care you would offer to a friend. When you make a mistake or encounter a challenge, instead of beating yourself up, offer yourself words of kindness and understanding.

Learn from your experiences

Every experience we have, whether positive or negative, offers us an opportunity to learn and grow. By reflecting on our experiences, we can gain valuable insights into ourselves and our emotions.

Take time to reflect on your experiences, both good and bad. Ask yourself what you learned from each experience and how it has helped you to grow. By learning from our experiences, we can deepen our emotional intelligence and become more self-aware.

In conclusion, quietness is a powerful tool for deepening our emotional intelligence. By practicing mindfulness, journaling, taking time for solitude, listening to our emotions, practicing empathy, cultivating self-compassion, and learning from our experiences, we can develop a greater understanding of ourselves and others. Quietness offers us the space to reflect, recharge, and cultivate our inner wisdom, which in turn can lead to greater self-discovery, personal growth, and lasting happiness. So, embrace the power of quietness and unlock your emotional intelligence today!

20: The Benefits of Sleep and Quietness

In today's fast-paced world, it can be challenging to find a moment of peace and quiet. We are constantly bombarded with noise and distractions, from the buzz of our phones to the chatter of colleagues in the workplace. Many of us may even feel guilty for taking a break from our busy schedules to relax and unwind. However, the truth is that rest and relaxation are essential for our mental, physical, and emotional well-being. In this chapter, we will explore the benefits of sleep and quietness and how they can transform our lives.

Sleep is one of the most fundamental human needs, yet many of us neglect it. According to the National Sleep Foundation, adults need seven to nine hours of sleep per night to function at their best. However, studies have shown that up to 30% of adults in the United States suffer from insomnia, a sleep disorder that makes it difficult to fall or stay asleep. Lack of sleep not only affects our mood and productivity but can also have serious health consequences. Chronic sleep deprivation has been linked to obesity, diabetes, heart disease, and depression.

On the other hand, getting enough sleep can have numerous benefits for our physical and mental health. During sleep, our bodies repair and rejuvenate themselves. It also plays a vital role in memory consolidation, allowing us to retain and recall information more efficiently. Additionally, studies have shown that getting enough sleep can improve our mood, reduce stress, and enhance our creativity and problem-solving abilities.

However, getting enough sleep is only part of the equation. We also need to make time for quietness, which can be just as essential for our well-being. Quietness allows us to disconnect from the noise and distractions of daily life and focus on ourselves. It gives us the opportunity to reflect, recharge, and gain perspective on our lives. However, many of us may find it challenging to find quietness in our daily lives.

In our modern world, quietness has become a rare commodity. We are constantly bombarded with noise and distractions, from the buzz of our phones to the chatter of colleagues in the workplace. Even our leisure time is often filled with noise, from the blaring of televisions to the roar of traffic outside our windows. However, the benefits of quietness are numerous.

First and foremost, quietness allows us to reduce stress and anxiety. The constant noise and stimulation of our daily lives can take a toll on our mental health, leaving us feeling overwhelmed and frazzled. However, taking a few moments to disconnect from the noise and focus on our breath can be incredibly calming and soothing. Even just a few minutes of quietness each day can have a significant impact on our mood and well-being.

Quietness also allows us to improve our focus and concentration. When we are constantly bombarded with distractions, it can be challenging to stay focused on the task at hand. However, taking a few moments to quiet our minds and eliminate distractions can help us stay on track and be more productive.

In addition, quietness can also be an essential tool for personal growth and self-discovery. By taking the time to reflect and gain perspective on our lives, we can gain insight into our values, goals, and desires. We can also identify areas for growth and improvement, allowing us to become the best versions of ourselves.

So, how can we incorporate more sleep and quietness into our lives? There are numerous strategies we can use, from developing a consistent sleep schedule to setting aside time each day for quiet reflection. Here are some tips to get started:

Create a sleep-friendly environment: Make sure your bedroom is dark, quiet, and cool to promote restful sleep.

Stick to a sleep schedule: Go to bed and wake up at the same time every day, even on weekends.

Limit screen time before bed: The blue light emitted by electronic devices can disrupt our sleep-wake cycle. Try to avoid using screens for at least an hour before bed.

Practice relaxation techniques: Deep breathing, meditation, and yoga can help calm your mind and promote relaxation.

Set aside time for quietness: Whether it's a few minutes in the morning or an hour before bed, make time each day for quiet reflection and self-care.

Take breaks throughout the day: If possible, take short breaks throughout the day to disconnect from work and recharge your batteries.

Spend time in nature: Nature has a calming effect on the mind and body. Take a walk in the park or go for a hike to experience the benefits of quietness in nature.

Practice mindfulness: Mindfulness involves focusing on the present moment and accepting it without judgment. It can be an effective way to reduce stress and increase self-awareness.

Consider professional help: If you are struggling with sleep or mental health issues, consider seeking help from a professional.

In conclusion, sleep and quietness are essential for our physical, mental, and emotional well-being. By making time for rest and relaxation, we can reduce stress, improve our focus and concentration, and promote personal growth and self-discovery. Incorporating these practices into our daily lives may require some effort and discipline, but the benefits are well worth it. So, let's embrace the power of quietness and unlock its potential for lasting happiness and well-being.

21: Quietness in Relationships: Strengthening Your Connection with Others

As human beings, we are social creatures. We thrive on connection and relationships with others. However, in our fast-paced world, we often overlook the importance of quietness in relationships. We live in a world where we are constantly connected, where the noise never stops. Our phones are always buzzing, our schedules are packed with activities and events, and we find ourselves constantly surrounded by people. In the midst of all this noise, it can be difficult to find the time and space for quietness in our relationships. Yet, it is precisely this quietness that can strengthen our connections with others and bring us lasting happiness.

Quietness in relationships means taking the time to listen deeply to others, to connect with them on a deeper level, and to create space for meaningful conversations. It means putting aside our phones, our to-do lists, and our busy schedules to be fully present with the people we care about. When we take the time to be quiet and listen, we create space for understanding, empathy, and compassion. We allow ourselves to truly connect with others and build meaningful relationships that can withstand the test of time.

One of the keys to developing quietness in relationships is to practice active listening. This means listening with intention and attention, rather than just waiting for our turn to speak. When we practice active listening, we not only hear the words that are being spoken, but we also pay attention to the non-verbal cues, such as tone of voice, facial expressions, and body language. By doing so, we gain a deeper understanding of the other person's thoughts, feelings, and perspectives, and we are better able to respond in a thoughtful and empathetic manner.

Another way to cultivate quietness in relationships is to create space for meaningful conversations. This means setting aside time to have deep, thoughtful conversations with the people we care about, rather than just engaging in small talk or idle chitchat. When we create space for meaningful conversations, we allow ourselves to explore deeper issues and ideas, to share our hopes and dreams, and to build a deeper connection with others.

In addition to active listening and meaningful conversations, another key to developing quietness in relationships is to practice empathy and compassion. Empathy means putting ourselves in the other person's shoes, trying to understand their perspective and their feelings. Compassion means showing kindness and understanding towards others, even when we disagree with them or when they have hurt us in some way. By practicing empathy and compassion, we create a safe space for others to share their thoughts and feelings, and we build stronger, more meaningful relationships.

Finally, developing quietness in relationships means learning to embrace solitude. This may seem counterintuitive, as we often think of relationships as being about connection and togetherness. However, solitude is an essential part of any healthy relationship. When we take time to be alone, we allow ourselves to reflect on our thoughts and feelings, to recharge our batteries, and to cultivate a sense of inner peace. This, in turn, makes us better able to be present and fully engaged with the people we care about when we are with them.

In conclusion, quietness in relationships is about taking the time to truly connect with others, to listen deeply, to engage in meaningful conversations, and to practice empathy and compassion. It is about creating space for understanding, empathy, and compassion, and about cultivating a sense of inner peace and solitude that allows us to be fully present with others. By developing quietness in our relationships, we can build stronger, more meaningful connections with the people we care about, and we can find lasting happiness and fulfillment in our lives.

22: Parenting with Quietness: Helping Children Thrive in a Busy World

In a world that is increasingly noisy, fast-paced, and demanding, it can be challenging to find moments of peace and quiet. However, as adults, we have learned the importance of taking time for ourselves, unplugging from technology, and embracing the stillness of solitude. But what about our children? How can we teach them the value of quietness and help them thrive in a world that often feels overwhelming?

Parenting with quietness is not about raising children who are silent, introverted, or detached from the world around them. Instead, it is about instilling in them the skills and tools to navigate the noise and distractions of modern life while remaining connected to their inner selves. Here are some proven strategies and insights that can help you raise children who embrace quietness and find inner peace in a busy world.

Create a Quiet Space

One of the simplest ways to encourage quietness in children

is to create a dedicated space for them to retreat to when they need a break from the chaos of daily life. This could be a cozy reading nook, a meditation corner, or simply a comfortable chair in a quiet room. The key is to make it a place where your child can feel safe, calm, and free from distractions.

Encourage Mindfulness

Mindfulness is the practice of being fully present and engaged in the moment, without judgment or distraction. Teaching your child mindfulness techniques can help them stay focused, reduce stress and anxiety, and improve their overall well-being. There are many ways to introduce mindfulness to children, including guided meditations, breathing exercises, and yoga.

Limit Screen Time

Technology has become an integral part of modern life, but too much screen time can have negative effects on children's health and well-being. Studies have linked excessive screen time to sleep problems, obesity, and even lower academic performance. Encourage your child to spend more time outdoors, engage in physical activities, and interact with the world around them.

Encourage Creativity

Creative expression is a powerful tool for promoting quietness and inner peace in children. Whether it's painting, writing, or playing music, encouraging your child to explore their creative side can help them develop a deeper sense of self-awareness and mindfulness. It can also be a great way for them to express their emotions and cope with stress.

Model Quietness

Children learn by example, so it's essential to model the behavior you want to see in them. Make time for quietness in your own life, whether it's reading a book, taking a walk in nature, or simply sitting in stillness. By showing your child the value of quietness, you can help them develop a lifelong appreciation for the power of solitude and inner peace.

Encourage Gratitude

Gratitude is a powerful emotion that can help children focus on the positive aspects of their lives, even in the face of adversity. Encourage your child to take a few moments each day to reflect on the things they are grateful for, whether it's a sunny day, a loving family, or a good meal. This simple practice can help them cultivate a more positive outlook on life and reduce stress and anxiety.

Teach Empathy

Empathy is the ability to understand and share the feelings of others, and it is a critical skill for building strong relationships and fostering a sense of community. Encourage your child to practice empathy by listening to others, showing kindness and compassion, and considering the perspectives of those around them. By teaching your child to see the world through the eyes of others, you can help them develop a deeper sense of connection and understanding.

In conclusion, parenting with quietness is about creating an environment that fosters self-awareness, mindfulness, and inner peace. By teaching your child the value of solitude, gratitude, empathy, and creativity, you can help them thrive in a busy and noisy world while remaining connected to their inner selves. It's important to remember that these skills take time to develop, and it's okay for your child to make mistakes and struggle along the way. Be patient and supportive, and offer guidance and encouragement when needed.

Another important aspect of parenting with quietness is recognizing the unique needs and personalities of your child. Some children may naturally gravitate towards quiet activities like reading or drawing, while others may prefer more active pursuits. It's important to encourage your child's individual interests and allow them to explore and discover what brings them joy and peace.

It's also important to set boundaries and establish routines that promote quietness and mindfulness in your home. This could include designated times for technology-free activities, family meditation or mindfulness practices, or simply turning off the TV during meal times. These small changes can have a big impact on your child's well-being and can help create a more peaceful and harmonious home environment.

Finally, it's important to seek support and guidance as needed. Parenting can be challenging, and there may be times when you feel overwhelmed or unsure of how to help your child navigate the complexities of modern life. Consider reaching out to other parents, joining a parenting support group, or seeking advice from a qualified professional. Remember, you don't have to do it alone.

In conclusion, parenting with quietness is about creating a nurturing and supportive environment that promotes self-awareness, mindfulness, and inner peace in children. By teaching your child the value of solitude, gratitude, empathy, and creativity, you can help them thrive in a noisy and fast-paced world while remaining connected to their inner selves. Remember to be patient, supportive, and adaptable, and don't be afraid to seek guidance and support when needed. With these tools and insights, you can help your child discover the power of quietness and unlock their full potential for self-discovery, personal growth, and lasting happiness.

23: Quietness and Productivity: How Slowing Down Can Help You Achieve More

In today's fast-paced world, productivity has become synonymous with success. The more we do, the more we achieve, and the more we achieve, the happier we are supposed to be. However, the truth is that this approach to life can leave us feeling exhausted, overwhelmed, and disconnected from ourselves. We are so busy chasing our goals that we forget to take a moment to reflect on our lives and what we really want. In this chapter, we will explore how slowing down and embracing quietness can help us become more productive, focused, and fulfilled in our lives.

The Power of Quietness

In a world that is constantly bombarding us with information, quietness has become a rare commodity. It is easy to get caught up in the noise of daily life, and we may not even realize how much it is affecting us. Research has shown that exposure to noise pollution can lead to high levels of stress, decreased productivity, and even health problems like hypertension and heart disease.

On the other hand, quietness has been proven to have numerous benefits for our mental and physical health. When we take time to be quiet, our brainwaves shift from the busy beta state to the more relaxed alpha and theta states. This shift promotes relaxation, creativity, and a sense of well-being. It also helps us to focus and concentrate better, which can lead to increased productivity.

The Link Between Quietness and Productivity

In a culture that values busyness and achievement, it may seem counterintuitive to suggest that slowing down can actually make us more productive. However, research has shown that taking breaks and allowing our minds to rest can actually improve our focus and concentration, leading to increased productivity in the long run.

One study found that taking a 15-minute break every hour can lead to a 30% increase in productivity. Another study found that taking a walk in nature can improve cognitive function and creativity, leading to better problem-solving and decision-making abilities.

When we are constantly rushing from one task to another,

our brains don't have time to process the information we are taking in. This can lead to a sense of overwhelm and make it difficult to concentrate on the task at hand. By taking time to be quiet and reflect, we give our brains the opportunity to process and organize the information, making it easier to focus and be productive when we return to our tasks.

Quietness also allows us to tap into our intuition and inner wisdom. When we are constantly distracted by external stimuli, it can be difficult to hear the quiet voice inside us that is guiding us towards our true purpose. Taking time to be quiet and reflect can help us tune into that inner voice and gain clarity about our goals and priorities.

How to Embrace Quietness for Increased Productivity

Now that we understand the link between quietness and productivity, let's explore some practical strategies for incorporating quietness into our daily lives.

Start your day with quiet time

Instead of jumping right into your to-do list first thing in the morning, take some time to be quiet and reflect. This could be through meditation, journaling, or simply sitting in silence with a cup of tea. Starting your day with quiet time sets a positive tone for the rest of the day and helps you to approach your tasks with greater focus and clarity.

Take breaks throughout the day

As we mentioned earlier, taking breaks throughout the day can actually increase your productivity. Set a timer for 25-30 minutes of work, followed by a 5-10 minute break. During your break, step away from your computer and do something restorative, like taking a walk, stretching, or simply closing your eyes and breathing deeply.

Create a quiet workspace

If possible, create a workspace that is free from distractions and noise. This could be a dedicated room or simply a corner of your home where you feel calm and focused. If you work in a busy office environment, consider using noise-cancelling headphones to block out distractions.

Practice mindfulness

Mindfulness is the practice of being fully present in the moment and observing your thoughts and feelings without judgment. By practicing mindfulness, you can become more aware of the distractions and patterns that are preventing you from being productive. You can also use mindfulness techniques, like deep breathing or body scanning, to help you relax and refocus during moments of stress or overwhelm.

Schedule time for quietness

Just like you schedule time for work tasks or appointments, make sure to schedule time for quietness in your daily routine. This could be a weekly yoga class, a daily meditation practice, or even a few minutes of quiet reflection before bed. By scheduling quiet time, you make it a priority in your life and ensure that you are taking the necessary steps to stay focused and productive.

Embrace solitude

Solitude is the state of being alone and can be a powerful tool for personal growth and reflection. Instead of always seeking out company or distractions, make an effort to spend time alone with your thoughts. This could be a solo hike in nature, a solo trip to a museum, or simply spending an evening at home with a good book. Embracing solitude allows you to connect with yourself and gain clarity about your goals and priorities.

Conclusion

In a world that values productivity and achievement above all else, it can be difficult to find the space for quietness and reflection. However, by embracing quietness, we can actually become more productive, focused, and fulfilled in our lives. By taking breaks, practicing mindfulness, and scheduling time for quietness, we can tap into our inner wisdom and connect with our true purpose. So, the next time you feel overwhelmed or stuck, try slowing down and embracing quietness. You may be surprised at how much it helps you achieve in the long run.

24: Balancing Quietness and Action: Finding Harmony in Life

Life is a balance of opposites. There is light and dark, happiness and sadness, joy and sorrow, and of course, action and quietness. Both action and quietness are necessary for a fulfilling and meaningful life. Action allows us to achieve our goals, to create, to connect with others, and to contribute to the world. Quietness, on the other hand, allows us to reflect, to recharge, to find inner peace, and to connect with ourselves.

But how can we find a balance between these two seemingly opposite states? How can we be both active and quiet in our lives? The answer lies in understanding the nature of action and quietness, and how they complement each other.

Action is the expression of our energy and creativity. It is the outward manifestation of our thoughts, desires, and intentions. Action allows us to make things happen, to accomplish our goals, and to create a better world. However, action also comes with its own set of challenges. It can be stressful, overwhelming, and exhausting, especially when we are constantly in a state of busyness and hustle.

24: BALANCING QUIETNESS AND ACTION: FINDING HARMONY IN LIFE

Quietness, on the other hand, is the state of being still, calm, and peaceful. It is the inward expression of our thoughts, feelings, and emotions. Quietness allows us to slow down, to reflect, and to find inner peace. However, quietness also has its own set of challenges. It can be uncomfortable, lonely, and sometimes even boring, especially when we are used to being constantly stimulated and entertained.

The key to finding balance between action and quietness is to understand that they are not mutually exclusive, but rather complementary. When we are in a state of quietness, we are able to recharge our energy and creativity, which allows us to approach our actions with more clarity, focus, and purpose. When we are in a state of action, we are able to express our energy and creativity, which allows us to experience a sense of accomplishment and fulfillment, and also provides us with opportunities for growth and learning.

The challenge, however, is to find the right balance between these two states. Too much action can lead to burnout and exhaustion, while too much quietness can lead to stagnation and lack of progress. Therefore, it is important to cultivate a healthy relationship between action and quietness, and to integrate both into our daily lives.

Here are some strategies that can help you balance action and quietness in your life:

Set clear boundaries: Set clear boundaries between your work and personal life, and between your active and quiet time. This will help you prioritize your time and energy, and ensure that you have enough space for both action and quietness in your life.

Schedule your quiet time: Make sure to schedule regular quiet time in your day or week. This can be in the form of meditation, yoga, reading, or any other activity that allows you to be still and calm. This will help you recharge your energy and creativity, and also provide you with a sense of peace and tranquility.

Practice mindfulness: Mindfulness is the practice of being present and aware in the moment. It can help you cultivate a sense of calm and clarity, and also help you manage stress and anxiety. Try to practice mindfulness throughout your day, whether you are in a state of action or quietness.

24: BALANCING QUIETNESS AND ACTION: FINDING HARMONY IN LIFE

Prioritize your tasks: Make sure to prioritize your tasks based on their importance and urgency. This will help you avoid feeling overwhelmed and stressed, and also ensure that you have enough time and energy for both action and quietness in your life.

Engage in meaningful activities: Engage in activities that are meaningful and fulfilling to you. This can be in the form of creative projects, volunteering, or spending time with loved ones. This will help you stay motivated and inspired, and also provide you with opportunities for personal growth and development.

Take breaks: Make sure to take regular breaks throughout your day or week, especially when you are in a state of action. This will help you recharge your energy and creativity, and also prevent burnout and exhaustion.

Connect with nature: Spend time in nature, whether it's going for a walk in the park, hiking in the mountains, or simply sitting in your backyard. Nature has a calming and soothing effect on our minds and bodies, and can help us find a sense of peace and tranquility.

24: BALANCING QUIETNESS AND ACTION: FINDING HARMONY IN LIFE

Embrace solitude: Embrace the power of solitude, and spend time alone with yourself. This can be in the form of journaling, reflection, or simply sitting in silence. Solitude allows us to connect with ourselves, and also provides us with opportunities for self-discovery and personal growth.

Practice gratitude: Practice gratitude on a daily basis, and focus on the things that you are thankful for in your life. Gratitude can help shift your perspective and mindset, and also provide you with a sense of peace and contentment.

Be present: Finally, make sure to be present and fully engaged in whatever you are doing, whether it's in a state of action or quietness. Being present allows us to fully experience and appreciate the moments in our lives, and also helps us cultivate a sense of mindfulness and awareness.

In conclusion, finding balance between action and quietness is essential for a fulfilling and meaningful life. By cultivating a healthy relationship between these two states, we can experience a sense of peace, contentment, and personal growth. So, embrace both action and quietness in your life, and find harmony in the balance between the two.

25: The Art of Saying No: Setting Boundaries and Finding Balance

In our fast-paced, always-connected world, it can be difficult to find the time and space to simply be still and quiet. Yet, the benefits of doing so are undeniable. Quietness, or the intentional practice of stillness and solitude, can help us find inner peace, clarity, and focus. It can also help us set boundaries, prioritize our time and energy, and ultimately, live a more fulfilling life.

One of the most important aspects of quietness is the ability to say no. Saying no is about setting boundaries and protecting our time, energy, and resources. It's about recognizing our limits and prioritizing our needs and values. Yet, many of us struggle with saying no. We fear that saying no will hurt others, make us seem selfish or rude, or cause us to miss out on opportunities.

But the truth is, saying no is an essential part of self-care and personal growth. Learning to say no can help us avoid burnout, reduce stress, and create more meaningful connections and experiences in our lives. In this chapter, we'll explore the art of saying no and how it can help us find balance and live a more intentional life.

25: THE ART OF SAYING NO: SETTING BOUNDARIES AND FINDING BALANCE

The Power of Saying No

Saying no is a powerful act of self-care. When we say no, we are setting boundaries and prioritizing our needs and values. We are saying "I value myself and my time, and I will not compromise my well-being for the sake of others." Saying no can help us avoid overcommitting, which can lead to burnout, stress, and even resentment. It can also help us create more meaningful connections and experiences in our lives, by allowing us to focus on what truly matters to us.

The Fear of Saying No

Despite the benefits of saying no, many of us struggle with it. We fear that saying no will hurt others, make us seem selfish or rude, or cause us to miss out on opportunities. We may also fear that saying no will lead to conflict or rejection. These fears can hold us back from setting boundaries and prioritizing our needs and values.

To overcome the fear of saying no, it's important to recognize that saying no is not a negative act. It's not about rejecting others or shutting them out. It's about creating a healthy balance in our lives and honoring our own needs and values. When we say no, we are saying "I value myself and my time, and I will not compromise my well-being for the sake of others." By reframing our mindset around saying no, we can begin to see it as a positive act of self-care and personal growth.

The Art of Saying No

Saying no is an art form, and like any art form, it takes practice to master. Here are some tips for saying no effectively and respectfully:

Be clear and concise: When saying no, be clear and concise in your communication. Use simple language and avoid being overly apologetic or defensive. For example, "Thank you for the invitation, but I won't be able to attend" is a clear and respectful way to decline an invitation.

Offer an explanation (if necessary): Sometimes, it may be helpful to offer an explanation for why you are saying no. This can help the other person understand your perspective and avoid any misunderstandings. However, it's important to remember that you don't owe anyone an explanation for your choices. If you choose to offer an explanation, keep it simple and honest. For example, "I'm currently focusing on other priorities right now" is a valid reason for saying no.

Offer an alternative (if possible): If you are unable to say yes to a request, but still want to show your support or interest, consider offering an alternative. For example, "I can't make it to the meeting tomorrow, but I'd be happy to catch up with you next week to discuss the project further."

Be firm but respectful: It's important to be firm in your decision to say no, but also to be respectful of the other person's feelings. Avoid being dismissive or rude, and instead, offer your response in a kind and courteous manner.

Practice self-reflection: Before saying yes or no to a request, take some time to reflect on your own needs and values. Ask yourself, "Does this align with my priorities?" "Will this compromise my well-being?" "Am I saying yes out of obligation or guilt?" By practicing self-reflection, you can make more intentional and empowered decisions about how to use your time and energy.

The Benefits of Saying No

25: THE ART OF SAYING NO: SETTING BOUNDARIES AND FINDING BALANCE

Learning to say no can have a profound impact on our lives. Here are just a few of the benefits of setting boundaries and prioritizing our needs and values:

Reduced stress and burnout: Saying no can help us avoid overcommitting and taking on too much. This can lead to reduced stress and burnout, and allow us to focus on what truly matters to us.

Increased self-esteem and self-worth: Saying no is an act of self-care and self-respect. By prioritizing our needs and values, we can increase our self-esteem and self-worth.

Improved relationships: When we say no, we are being honest and authentic with ourselves and others. This can lead to more meaningful connections and deeper relationships.

More intentional living: By setting boundaries and saying no to things that don't align with our priorities, we can live a more intentional and purposeful life.

In Conclusion

Saying no is an essential part of self-care and personal growth. It's about setting boundaries, prioritizing our needs and values, and ultimately, living a more fulfilling life. By learning the art of saying no, we can avoid burnout, reduce stress, and create more meaningful connections and experiences in our lives. So, the next time you're faced with a request that doesn't align with your priorities, remember that saying no is a positive act of self-care and personal growth.

26: Dealing with Distractions: Strategies for Quieting Your Mind

Distractions are everywhere in today's world, from social media notifications to the constant bombardment of advertisements. We are constantly being pulled away from our tasks and goals by these distractions, leaving us feeling stressed and overwhelmed. However, by learning how to quiet our minds and eliminate distractions, we can achieve greater focus, productivity, and inner peace. In this chapter, we'll explore some proven strategies for dealing with distractions and finding quietness in our daily lives.

Understand the Power of Mindfulness

One of the most effective ways to quiet your mind and eliminate distractions is to practice mindfulness. Mindfulness is the practice of paying attention to the present moment, without judgment or distraction. By becoming more aware of your thoughts and emotions, you can learn to let go of distractions and focus on what's important.

To practice mindfulness, start by finding a quiet place to sit and focus on your breath. As you inhale and exhale, pay attention to the sensation of the air moving in and out of your body. Whenever your mind starts to wander, gently bring your focus back to your breath. This simple exercise can help you become more aware of your thoughts and emotions, and give you the tools you need to let go of distractions.

Create a Distraction-Free Environment

Another effective strategy for dealing with distractions is to create a distraction-free environment. This can involve making small changes to your workspace or daily routine to reduce the number of distractions you encounter. For example, you might turn off your phone or computer notifications during certain times of the day, or block distracting websites from your browser.

Another effective strategy is to create a dedicated workspace that's free from distractions. This might involve setting up a quiet room in your home or finding a quiet corner in your workplace where you can focus on your work without interruption. By creating a distraction-free environment, you can eliminate many of the distractions that pull you away from your goals and tasks.

26: DEALING WITH DISTRACTIONS: STRATEGIES FOR QUIETING YOUR MIND

Practice Digital Minimalism

In today's digital age, it's easy to become overwhelmed by the constant barrage of information and notifications. However, by practicing digital minimalism, you can reduce the amount of time you spend on your devices and free up more time for quiet reflection and self-care.

Digital minimalism involves being intentional about the time you spend on your devices, and focusing on activities that bring you joy and fulfillment. This might involve taking a break from social media or email, and instead spending time reading, meditating, or spending time with loved ones. By prioritizing your time and energy, you can reduce the amount of time you spend on distractions, and focus on what's truly important.

Embrace Solitude

Finally, one of the most powerful strategies for dealing with distractions is to embrace solitude. Solitude involves spending time alone, without the distractions of other people or technology. By spending time alone, you can reflect on your thoughts and emotions, and gain a deeper understanding of yourself and your place in the world.

To embrace solitude, start by finding a quiet place to spend time alone. This might involve taking a walk in nature, reading a book in a quiet room, or simply sitting in silence for a few minutes each day. By embracing solitude, you can learn to quiet your mind and eliminate distractions, and find greater inner peace and happiness.

In conclusion, dealing with distractions is essential for finding quietness in today's fast-paced world. By practicing mindfulness, creating a distraction-free environment, practicing digital minimalism, and embracing solitude, you can reduce the amount of time you spend on distractions, and focus on what's truly important. So take the time to implement these strategies in your daily life, and unlock the power of quietness for greater self-discovery, personal growth, and lasting happiness!

27: Embracing Uncertainty: Finding Peace in Life's Challenges

Life is full of uncertainties. No matter how well we plan and prepare, there are always unexpected events that can shake us to our core. These events can come in many forms - a sudden illness, a job loss, the end of a relationship, or a natural disaster. Whatever the challenge may be, it can leave us feeling lost, helpless, and uncertain about what the future holds.

But what if we could learn to embrace uncertainty? What if we could see life's challenges as opportunities for growth and transformation? In this chapter, we will explore the power of embracing uncertainty and how it can help us find peace in life's challenges.

First, it's important to understand that uncertainty is a natural part of life. We can't control everything that happens to us, but we can control how we respond to it. When we resist uncertainty, we create more stress and anxiety for ourselves. We become stuck in a cycle of worry and fear, which can lead to physical and emotional exhaustion.

But when we embrace uncertainty, we open ourselves up to

new possibilities and experiences. We become more resilient and adaptable, and we learn to trust in our own abilities to handle whatever comes our way. Here are some strategies to help you embrace uncertainty and find peace in life's challenges:

Practice mindfulness: Mindfulness is the practice of being fully present in the moment, without judgment or distraction. When we practice mindfulness, we become more aware of our thoughts and emotions, and we can respond to them with greater clarity and calmness. By staying present and focused, we can reduce our anxiety and find greater peace in the face of uncertainty.

Cultivate gratitude: Gratitude is the practice of focusing on the good in our lives, even amidst the challenges and difficulties. When we cultivate gratitude, we shift our perspective from scarcity to abundance. We begin to see the blessings and opportunities in our lives, even when things aren't going as we had hoped.

Develop a growth mindset: A growth mindset is the belief that we can learn and grow from our challenges and failures. When we develop a growth mindset, we see challenges as opportunities for learning and growth, rather than as threats to our self-esteem. We become more resilient and adaptable, and we can find meaning and purpose in even the most difficult circumstances.

Connect with others: When we face uncertainty, it's important to lean on the support of others. We don't have to face our challenges alone. By connecting with others, we can share our experiences, gain new perspectives, and receive emotional support. This can help us feel less isolated and more hopeful about the future.

Take action: While uncertainty can feel overwhelming, taking action can help us regain a sense of control and empowerment. We may not be able to control everything, but we can take small steps to move forward in the direction of our goals and values. By taking action, we can build momentum and create a sense of progress, even in the face of uncertainty.

In conclusion, embracing uncertainty is not always easy, but it is a powerful way to find peace in life's challenges. By practicing mindfulness, cultivating gratitude, developing a growth mindset, connecting with others, and taking action, we can learn to navigate life's uncertainties with greater ease and resilience. Instead of fearing uncertainty, we can embrace it as a natural part of life's journey and trust in our own abilities to navigate it with grace and courage.

28: The Power of Forgiveness: Quieting the Noise of Resentment

Forgiveness is a powerful tool for unlocking the full potential of quietness in our lives. It allows us to let go of the pain and resentment that often hold us back and keep us from achieving true inner peace and happiness. In this chapter, we will explore the many benefits of forgiveness and learn how to harness its power to transform our lives.

What is Forgiveness?

Forgiveness is the act of letting go of anger, resentment, or bitterness towards someone who has wronged us. It is a conscious decision to release the negative emotions and thoughts that have been holding us back and move on with our lives. Forgiveness does not mean forgetting or excusing the wrong that was done, nor does it require reconciliation with the person who caused the hurt. It simply means acknowledging the pain, letting go of the negative emotions, and moving forward in a positive and productive way.

The Benefits of Forgiveness

Forgiveness has many benefits, both physical and emotional. When we forgive, we release the negative emotions that are often associated with hurt and pain. This can lead to a decrease in stress, anxiety, and depression, as well as an increase in overall well-being and happiness.

Forgiveness can also improve our relationships with others. When we let go of our anger and resentment towards someone, we open ourselves up to the possibility of reconciliation and healing. Forgiveness can help to restore trust, strengthen relationships, and promote a sense of unity and understanding.

Forgiveness can also help us to grow as individuals. By letting go of our negative emotions, we create space for positive emotions like love, compassion, and empathy. We become more self-aware and mindful of our own thoughts and feelings, and we learn to view the world from a more positive and productive perspective.

How to Forgive

Forgiveness is not always easy, but it is always worth it. Here are some strategies that can help you to forgive and move forward:

28: THE POWER OF FORGIVENESS: QUIETING THE NOISE OF RESENTMENT

Acknowledge the hurt: Before you can forgive someone, you need to acknowledge the hurt that was caused. This may involve expressing your feelings to the person who wronged you or simply acknowledging your own pain.

Practice empathy: Try to put yourself in the other person's shoes and understand their perspective. This can help you to see the situation in a different light and find common ground.

Let go of the negative emotions: This is often the most difficult part of forgiveness, but it is essential for moving forward. Take some time to reflect on your feelings and try to release the anger, resentment, and bitterness that you may be holding onto.

Focus on the positive: Instead of dwelling on the negative, try to focus on the positive aspects of the situation. Look for opportunities for growth and learning, and embrace the possibility of reconciliation and healing.

Practice self-care: Forgiveness can be a challenging process, and it is important to take care of yourself during this time. Practice self-care activities like exercise, meditation, or spending time with loved ones.

Conclusion

Forgiveness is a powerful tool for unlocking the full potential of quietness in our lives. By letting go of negative emotions and focusing on the positive, we can experience greater levels of inner peace, happiness, and personal growth. Remember that forgiveness is a process, and it may take time and effort to fully let go of hurt and resentment. However, the benefits of forgiveness are well worth the effort, and can lead to a more fulfilling and meaningful life.

29: Quietness and Healing: Restoring Balance and Wellness

Introduction

In the hustle and bustle of modern life, we rarely take a moment to slow down and reflect. Our lives are filled with noise, distractions, and constant stimulation. It's easy to get caught up in the chaos and lose sight of what really matters. But what if I told you that there is power in quietness? What if I told you that by embracing solitude, you can find inner peace, restore balance, and transform your life? This chapter will explore the healing power of quietness and how it can help us find wellness and balance in our lives.

The Healing Power of Quietness

For many of us, the idea of sitting in silence for even a few minutes can seem daunting. We're so used to the constant noise of our lives that the thought of being alone with our thoughts can be overwhelming. But the truth is, quietness has the power to heal us in ways that nothing else can.

When we take the time to be still and quiet, we give ourselves the space to breathe and reflect. We allow ourselves to process our thoughts and emotions, to let go of stress and anxiety, and to find clarity and focus. By tuning out the noise and distractions of the world, we can tune into our inner selves and connect with our truest desires.

Quietness can also help us connect with the present moment. When we're constantly on the go, it's easy to get caught up in what's next and forget about what's happening right now. But by slowing down and being present, we can appreciate the beauty and wonder of the world around us. We can find joy in the small moments, and we can cultivate a sense of gratitude for all that we have.

The Importance of Self-Care

In order to truly embrace quietness and find healing, it's important to prioritize self-care. This means taking the time to care for our physical, emotional, and mental well-being. It means carving out time in our busy schedules to do the things that nourish us and fill us up.

Self-care can take many forms. For some, it might mean taking a long bath or going for a walk in nature. For others, it might mean practicing yoga or meditation. Whatever it looks like for you, it's important to make self-care a priority.

When we take care of ourselves, we give ourselves the energy and resources we need to show up fully in our lives. We become more resilient, more grounded, and more able to handle whatever comes our way. By prioritizing self-care, we also send a powerful message to ourselves and those around us: that we are worthy of love and care, and that we value our well-being above all else.

Finding Balance in a Busy World

One of the biggest challenges of modern life is finding balance. We're constantly bombarded with demands and distractions, and it can be hard to know how to prioritize our time and energy. But by embracing quietness and prioritizing self-care, we can find a sense of balance and wellness that is sustainable and nourishing.

One way to find balance is to set boundaries. This means being clear about what we will and won't tolerate in our lives, and making choices that honor our priorities and values. It means saying no to things that don't serve us, and yes to things that bring us joy and fulfillment.

Another way to find balance is to cultivate a sense of gratitude. When we focus on all that we have rather than what we lack, we shift our perspective and become more content with our lives. We become less focused on external validation and more focused on the things that truly matter.

Conclusion

Quietness has the power to heal us in ways that nothing else can. By embracing solitude and prioritizing self-care, we can find inner peace, restore balance, and transform our lives. It's not always easy to make time for quietness in a world that values busyness and productivity, but it's essential if we want to live lives that are fulfilling and meaningful.

Ultimately, finding healing through quietness is a journey that requires patience, persistence, and self-compassion. It's not a quick fix or a one-size-fits-all solution, but rather a process of discovery and growth that unfolds over time. It's about learning to listen to ourselves, trust our instincts, and honor our needs.

If you're feeling overwhelmed or burnt out, consider taking some time to sit in quietness and reflect on what you need to feel well and balanced. Whether it's a few minutes of meditation each day or a weekend retreat in nature, there are many ways to embrace solitude and find healing. By prioritizing quietness and self-care, we can create lives that are centered, grounded, and full of joy.

30: Quietness and Aging: Navigating Life Transitions with Grace

As we age, we face many transitions and changes in our lives. Whether it's retiring from a career, becoming an empty nester, or dealing with health issues, these transitions can be difficult to navigate. It's easy to feel overwhelmed and unsure of what the future holds.

However, embracing the power of quietness can help us navigate these transitions with grace and ease. Quietness is not just about being silent, it's about creating a space for reflection, introspection, and inner peace. When we embrace quietness, we can connect with our inner selves, find clarity, and discover new opportunities and possibilities.

Retirement is one of the most significant transitions we face as we age. For many, retirement represents a time to slow down and enjoy life. However, for others, retirement can be a source of anxiety and uncertainty. After spending years in a career, it can be challenging to adjust to a new lifestyle without the structure and routine of work.

Incorporating quietness into your retirement can help you find peace and purpose in this new chapter of life. Take the time to reflect on what you want to do with your newfound freedom. What hobbies have you always wanted to try? What places have you always wanted to visit? Use quietness to connect with your passions and explore new interests.

Another significant transition we face as we age is becoming an empty nester. After years of raising children, it can be challenging to adjust to a quieter home. However, this is an excellent opportunity to reconnect with your partner and rediscover your identity outside of parenthood.

Quietness can help you connect with your inner self and find clarity in this new phase of life. Take the time to reflect on who you are and what you want out of this next chapter. What goals do you have for yourself? What experiences do you want to have? Use quietness to connect with your desires and create a plan for achieving them.

Health issues are another common transition we face as we age. Whether it's a chronic illness or a sudden health crisis, dealing with health issues can be challenging both physically and emotionally. Quietness can help you find peace and strength during these difficult times.

30: QUIETNESS AND AGING: NAVIGATING LIFE TRANSITIONS WITH GRACE

Take the time to connect with your inner self and find peace in the present moment. Use quietness to meditate, journal, or simply sit in silence. Allow yourself to process your emotions and find acceptance in the situation. Use quietness to connect with your strength and resilience, and find ways to make the most of each day.

In conclusion, embracing quietness can help us navigate the transitions and changes we face as we age. By creating a space for reflection, introspection, and inner peace, we can find clarity, purpose, and strength in any situation. Whether it's retirement, becoming an empty nester, or dealing with health issues, quietness can help us find grace and ease in these transitions.

31: The Power of Community: Finding Quietness in Connection with Others

In a world that constantly emphasizes the importance of individualism and self-reliance, it can be easy to forget the power of community. However, the truth is that humans are social creatures by nature, and connecting with others is essential for our well-being. In fact, research has shown that social isolation can be as damaging to our health as smoking or obesity.

But what about those of us who crave quietness and solitude? Is it possible to find peace and connection with others at the same time? The answer is yes, and in this chapter, we'll explore how community can be a powerful tool for finding quietness and inner peace.

First, it's important to understand that community doesn't have to mean constant noise and stimulation. In fact, many people who prioritize quietness and solitude still find immense value in connecting with others in meaningful ways. It's all about finding a balance that works for you.

One way to do this is by seeking out like-minded individuals who share your values and interests. Whether it's a meditation group, a book club, or a hiking club, there are countless opportunities to connect with others who appreciate quietness and the power of stillness. These groups can provide a sense of belonging and connection, without overwhelming you with too much noise or stimulation.

Of course, finding a community that resonates with you isn't always easy. It may require some trial and error, and you may have to step outside of your comfort zone to find the right fit. But once you do, the benefits can be enormous.

For example, being part of a community can help you stay motivated and accountable in your personal growth journey. When you surround yourself with others who share your goals, it's easier to stay on track and push yourself to be your best self.

Additionally, being part of a community can help you gain new perspectives and insights. When you connect with others who come from different backgrounds and experiences, you're exposed to new ideas and ways of thinking that can expand your own worldview.

But perhaps most importantly, being part of a community can provide a sense of support and comfort during difficult times. When you're going through a challenging period in your life, having a group of people who understand and empathize with you can make all the difference.

Of course, it's important to remember that community isn't just about what you can get out of it. It's also about what you can give back. When you're part of a community, it's important to be an active and engaged member. This means showing up, participating, and being willing to contribute in meaningful ways.

Whether it's volunteering your time, sharing your expertise, or simply offering a listening ear, being a supportive and giving member of a community can be incredibly rewarding. Not only does it help you build deeper connections with others, but it also provides a sense of purpose and meaning in your life.

In conclusion, finding quietness in connection with others is not only possible, but it can be a powerful tool for personal growth and happiness. By seeking out like-minded individuals, staying open to new perspectives, and being an en-

gaged member of a community, you can experience the benefits of connection without sacrificing your need for
solitude and stillness.

So if you've been hesitant to connect with others because
you value quietness and solitude, remember that community doesn't have to mean constant noise and stimulation. With the right balance and mindset, you can find connection, support, and inner peace through the power of
community.

32: Quietness and Social Justice: Creating Change from a Place of Peace

In today's fast-paced, constantly connected world, it can be easy to forget the power of quietness. We are bombarded with noise, distractions, and demands on our time and attention, leaving little room for stillness and solitude. However, by embracing quietness, we can unlock a powerful tool for creating positive change in ourselves and in the world around us.

At first glance, quietness may seem at odds with the concept of social justice. After all, social justice requires action and advocacy, speaking out and standing up for what is right. But quietness is not about staying silent or passive in the face of injustice. Rather, it is a mindset that allows us to approach social justice from a place of inner peace and clarity, empowering us to create meaningful and lasting change.

One of the key benefits of quietness is the ability to tune out external distractions and focus inward. This can be especially important when it comes to issues of social justice, which can be overwhelming and emotionally charged. By taking the time to step back and reflect, we can gain perspective and clarity, identifying the root causes of injustice and developing effective strategies for addressing them.

Quietness can also help us cultivate a sense of compassion and empathy for those who are impacted by social injustice. When we are constantly surrounded by noise and distraction, it can be easy to become disconnected from the suffering of others. But by embracing stillness and solitude, we can develop a deeper understanding of the human experience and the ways in which systemic injustice can impact entire communities.

In addition, quietness can help us develop the resilience and patience needed to create real change. Social justice is often a slow and difficult process, requiring sustained effort over time. By cultivating a sense of inner peace and grounding ourselves in quietness, we can stay focused on our goals even in the face of setbacks and obstacles.

So how can we apply the principles of quietness to social justice advocacy? Here are a few strategies to consider:

Start with self-reflection. Before taking action, take the time to reflect on your own experiences and beliefs. What experiences have shaped your understanding of social justice? What biases or blind spots might be impacting your perspective? By taking an honest and reflective approach, you can ensure that your advocacy is grounded in a deep understanding of the issues at hand.

Practice active listening. When engaging with others, whether in person or online, make a conscious effort to truly listen to what they have to say. Resist the urge to respond immediately or interrupt, and instead take the time to fully understand their perspective. This can help build trust and empathy, laying the groundwork for productive dialogue and collaboration.

Cultivate a sense of stillness and presence. Whether through meditation, mindfulness, or other practices, find ways to cultivate a sense of inner peace and quietness. This can help you stay focused and grounded even in the midst of chaos and uncertainty.

Take action, but with intention. When taking action on issues of social justice, be intentional and strategic in your approach. Consider the long-term impact of your actions, and seek out opportunities to collaborate with others and build coalitions for change.

Practice self-care. Advocating for social justice can be emotionally taxing, and it's important to take care of yourself along the way. Make sure to prioritize rest, relaxation, and self-care practices that nourish your mind, body, and soul.

In conclusion, quietness is not about staying silent or passive in the face of injustice. Rather, it is a powerful tool for cultivating inner peace, empathy, and resilience – qualities that are essential for creating meaningful and lasting change. By embracing the power of quietness, we can approach social justice advocacy from a place of strength and clarity, transforming ourselves and the world around us in the process.

33: The Intersection of Quietness and Creativity: A Deep Dive

The power of creativity is often associated with loudness, chaos, and a constant stream of ideas flowing through our minds. We tend to think that being creative requires being extroverted, outgoing, and constantly surrounded by people and noise. However, as many great artists, writers, and thinkers have shown, creativity can also stem from a place of stillness, quietness, and solitude.

In fact, some of the most renowned artists in history were known for their introverted and introspective nature, spending long hours alone with their thoughts and ideas. Vincent van Gogh, Emily Dickinson, and Franz Kafka are just a few examples of creative geniuses who found solace and inspiration in quietness.

But how exactly does quietness intersect with creativity? And how can we tap into this power to unleash our own creative potential? In this chapter, we will explore the answers to these questions and discover the transformative effects of embracing the power of quietness in our creative endeavors.

The Benefits of Quietness for Creativity

33: THE INTERSECTION OF QUIETNESS AND CREATIVITY: A DEEP DIVE

First, let's explore the many ways in which quietness can benefit our creative processes.

Reduced Distractions: In a world full of distractions and interruptions, finding a quiet space and time to focus can be a game-changer for our creativity. When we remove the noise and chaos of our surroundings, we allow ourselves to fully immerse in our thoughts and ideas, without the constant pull of external stimuli.

Enhanced Focus: When our minds are not constantly bombarded with external input, we can focus more deeply on our own thoughts and ideas. This heightened focus can lead to more clarity, deeper insights, and a stronger connection to our creative vision.

Increased Introspection: Quietness allows us to turn inward and explore our own thoughts, emotions, and experiences. This introspection can lead to deeper self-awareness and a better understanding of the unique perspectives and insights we bring to our creative work.

Improved Memory and Cognitive Function: Studies have shown that quietness can improve our memory and cognitive function by reducing stress and anxiety, increasing oxygen flow to the brain, and enhancing neural connectivity. These benefits can lead to more efficient and effective creative processes.

Greater Emotional Regulation: Emotions play a significant role in creativity, and quietness can help us regulate our emotions and access deeper levels of empathy and compassion. By quieting the noise of our surroundings, we can tune into our own emotional experiences and connect more authentically with our creative vision.

How to Embrace Quietness in Creative Work

Now that we understand the benefits of quietness for creativity, let's explore some practical strategies for embracing quietness in our creative work.

Find a Quiet Space: Whether it's a secluded room in your home or a park bench in a quiet corner of a park, finding a space where you can escape the noise and distractions of your surroundings is essential for tapping into the power of quietness. Make it a priority to carve out time and space for quiet reflection and creative work.

33: THE INTERSECTION OF QUIETNESS AND CREATIVITY: A DEEP DIVE

Turn off Distractions: In addition to finding a quiet space, make sure to turn off any distractions that could pull you out of your creative zone. This could mean turning off your phone, closing your email, or even putting up a "do not disturb" sign on your door.

Practice Mindfulness: Mindfulness is a powerful tool for embracing quietness and connecting with our inner thoughts and experiences. Try incorporating mindfulness practices like meditation, deep breathing, or yoga into your creative routine to enhance your focus and reduce stress and anxiety.

Experiment with Silence: While total silence is not always possible or desirable, experimenting with periods of silence can be a great way to tap into the power of quietness. Try spending a few minutes in complete silence before starting your creative work, or take breaks throughout your creative process to sit in silence and reflect on your thoughts and ideas.

Embrace Solitude: Solitude is often viewed as a negative state, but in reality, it can be a powerful tool for creativity. When we are alone with our thoughts, we are free to explore our own perspectives and experiences without the influence of others. Try embracing moments of solitude in your creative work to tap into your own unique voice and vision.

Connect with Nature: Nature is a natural source of quietness and can be a great way to inspire creativity. Try taking a walk in the woods or sitting by a river and allow yourself to become fully immersed in the beauty and stillness of the natural world. You may find that this connection to nature helps to unlock new ideas and perspectives.

Find Inspiration in Quietness: Quietness can be a powerful source of inspiration for creative work. Whether it's a quiet moment of introspection or a moment of stillness in nature, try to tune into these moments of quietness and allow them to inspire your creative vision.

The Power of Quietness for Lasting Creativity

Embracing the power of quietness in our creative work can lead to profound transformations in our creative processes and outcomes. By reducing distractions, enhancing focus, and tapping into our own unique perspectives, we can unlock new levels of creativity and self-discovery.

33: THE INTERSECTION OF QUIETNESS AND CREATIVITY: A DEEP DIVE

But the benefits of quietness go beyond the creative process itself. Embracing quietness can also lead to lasting changes in our lives and well-being. By reducing stress and anxiety, improving cognitive function, and enhancing emotional regulation, quietness can help us to live happier, healthier, and more fulfilling lives.

So, whether you're a writer, artist, musician, or simply someone who wants to tap into their own creative potential, embracing the power of quietness is essential for unlocking your full creative potential. By finding a quiet space, turning off distractions, and embracing moments of introspection and solitude, you can tap into the transformative power of quietness and unlock new levels of creativity, self-discovery, and lasting happiness.

34: Quietness and Purpose: Discovering Your Passion and Life Mission

The search for purpose and meaning in life is one of the most fundamental quests of human existence. We all want to feel that our lives have a greater significance, that we are making a meaningful contribution to the world, and that we are fulfilling our potential. Yet, in today's fast-paced and noisy world, it can be difficult to find the time and space to reflect on what truly matters to us and to discover our life mission. That's where the power of quietness comes in.

Quietness is not simply the absence of noise or the absence of activity. It is a state of mind and a way of being that allows us to tap into our inner wisdom, connect with our deepest desires, and find clarity and purpose in life. When we cultivate a practice of quietness, we are able to slow down, tune out distractions, and listen to the voice of our intuition and inner guidance. In this chapter, we will explore how you can use the power of quietness to discover your passion and life mission.

Step 1: Create Space for Quietness

34: QUIETNESS AND PURPOSE: DISCOVERING YOUR PASSION AND LIFE MISSION

The first step in discovering your life mission is to create space for quietness in your life. This means carving out time in your day to be still, silent, and present. It might mean waking up a little earlier in the morning to meditate, taking a quiet walk in nature during your lunch break, or simply turning off your phone and sitting in silence for a few minutes each day.

Whatever form it takes, the key is to make quietness a priority in your life. This can be challenging at first, especially if you are used to a busy and noisy lifestyle. But with practice, you will begin to crave these moments of quietness and find that they become a source of energy and inspiration for you.

Step 2: Reflect on Your Passions and Values

Once you have created space for quietness in your life, the next step is to reflect on your passions and values. What are the things that you love to do? What activities bring you the most joy and fulfillment? What are the causes or issues that you feel most passionate about?

Take some time to write down your answers to these questions. Don't worry about being "practical" or "realistic" at this stage. This is a time for dreaming and exploring what truly matters to you.

In addition to your passions, it's also important to reflect on your values. What are the principles or beliefs that guide your life? What do you stand for? What are the qualities or virtues that you admire in others?

As you reflect on your passions and values, pay attention to any common themes or patterns that emerge. These can provide clues to your life mission and purpose.

Step 3: Connect with Your Inner Guidance

The next step in discovering your life mission is to connect with your inner guidance. This is the voice of your intuition and inner wisdom that can help you make important decisions and guide you on your path.

To connect with your inner guidance, it's important to quiet your mind and tune out distractions. This is where your practice of quietness comes in. Find a quiet and comfortable space where you won't be interrupted, and take a few deep breaths to relax your body and mind.

Then, simply ask a question or state an intention, and listen for the answer that comes from within. This might take the form of a thought, a feeling, or a physical sensation. Trust that your inner guidance is always there to support you, and that you have the wisdom and resources within you to find your way.

Step 4: Take Action and Experiment

The final step in discovering your life mission is to take action and experiment. This means trying out different things and seeing what resonates with you. It means taking risks and stepping out of your comfort zone to explore new possibilities. It means being open to failure and learning from your experiences.

As you begin to experiment, keep in mind that your life mission may not be a specific job or career path. It may be a broader sense of purpose or a set of values that you embody in all aspects of your life. For example, your mission may be to inspire others, to make a difference in your community, or to live a life of creativity and self-expression.

Whatever your mission may be, stay true to your passions

and values, and trust that the right opportunities will present themselves as you move forward. Be patient and persistent, and don't be afraid to ask for help or guidance along the way.

Conclusion

Discovering your passion and life mission is a lifelong journey, and it requires patience, self-reflection, and a willingness to embrace the power of quietness. By creating space for quietness in your life, reflecting on your passions and values, connecting with your inner guidance, and taking action and experimenting, you can unlock the full potential of your life and find lasting happiness and fulfillment.

Remember that your life mission is unique to you, and that it may evolve and change over time. Embrace the journey, stay true to yourself, and trust that you have everything you need within you to create a life of purpose, meaning, and joy.

35: Quietness and Lasting Happiness: A New Way of Being

The pursuit of happiness is an age-old quest that has been around since the beginning of time. Humans have always sought to find lasting happiness, the kind of happiness that endures even in the midst of challenges and difficulties. Yet, despite our best efforts, happiness seems to elude many of us.

We often look for happiness in external things, such as wealth, status, relationships, or possessions. We think that if we can just acquire enough of these things, we will be happy. But the truth is, happiness cannot be found in external things alone. It is an inside job, and it starts with embracing the power of quietness.

Quietness is the state of being calm, still, and peaceful. It is the absence of noise and distractions, and the presence of inner stillness and clarity. When we cultivate quietness in our lives, we are able to connect with our inner selves, our intuition, and our higher selves. We are able to find peace in the midst of chaos, and clarity in the midst of confusion.

Quietness is not just a state of mind, but a way of being. It is a lifestyle that we can choose to adopt, a way of living that allows us to tap into the deeper parts of ourselves and experience lasting happiness.

To embrace the power of quietness, we must first learn to quiet the mind. Our minds are constantly bombarded with thoughts, worries, and distractions. We are often so caught up in our own heads that we fail to notice the beauty of the world around us.

To quiet the mind, we can start by practicing mindfulness meditation. Mindfulness meditation is a practice of being fully present in the moment, without judgment or distraction. By focusing our attention on our breath or a specific object, we can calm the mind and bring ourselves into a state of inner stillness.

In addition to mindfulness meditation, we can also practice other forms of quietness, such as spending time in nature, taking long walks, or engaging in creative activities such as painting or writing. These activities allow us to quiet the mind and tap into our inner creativity and intuition.

Once we have cultivated a state of inner stillness and quietness, we can begin to explore the deeper parts of ourselves. We can ask ourselves important questions such as: Who am I? What do I really want in life? What are my deepest values and beliefs?

By exploring these questions, we can gain a greater sense of self-awareness and clarity. We can start to align our actions and decisions with our deepest values and beliefs, and live a life that is truly authentic and fulfilling.

Living a life of quietness and stillness does not mean that we must completely withdraw from the world. Rather, it means that we approach the world from a place of inner peace and clarity. We are able to navigate the ups and downs of life with grace and resilience, and find joy and meaning in the simple moments of everyday life.

In conclusion, the power of quietness is a transformative force that can help us unlock lasting happiness and fulfillment. By cultivating a state of inner stillness and clarity, we can tap into our deepest selves and live a life that is authentic, meaningful, and full of joy. So, take some time to quiet your mind, connect with your inner self, and embrace the power of quietness in your life. You will be amazed at the transformative effects it can have on your overall wellbeing and happiness.

36: Embracing Quietness as a Way of Life: Final Thoughts and Reflections

As we come to the end of this journey, it is important to reflect on the many insights and strategies we have explored together in this book. From the benefits of solitude and stillness, to the power of mindfulness and self-awareness, we have learned that quietness is not simply the absence of noise or activity, but a state of being that allows us to tap into our inner wisdom and strength.

The world we live in today is full of distractions, noise, and constant stimulation. It can be challenging to find a sense of peace and quiet in the midst of all this chaos. However, by embracing quietness as a way of life, we can discover a sense of calm and inner stillness that can transform our lives in powerful ways.

One of the key insights we have explored in this book is the importance of solitude. Many people fear being alone, believing that it will lead to boredom or loneliness. However, as we have learned, solitude can be a powerful tool for self-discovery and personal growth. By spending time alone, we can reflect on our thoughts, feelings, and experiences, and gain a deeper understanding of who we are and what we truly want from life.

Another important aspect of quietness is mindfulness. This practice involves being fully present in the moment, paying attention to our thoughts, feelings, and physical sensations without judgment. Mindfulness can help us to reduce stress and anxiety, improve our relationships, and increase our overall sense of well-being.

Self-awareness is also crucial to living a life of quietness. By becoming more aware of our thoughts, feelings, and behaviors, we can begin to identify patterns that may be holding us back, and make positive changes that allow us to live more fully and authentically.

Of course, embracing quietness as a way of life is not always easy. We may face resistance from those around us who do not understand or value the importance of stillness and solitude. We may also struggle with our own internal resistance, as we confront aspects of ourselves that we have been avoiding or denying.

However, the rewards of embracing quietness are worth the effort. By cultivating a sense of inner stillness and calm, we can experience greater clarity, creativity, and resilience. We can connect more deeply with ourselves and with others, and live our lives with greater purpose and meaning.

So how can we begin to embrace quietness as a way of life? Here are some final thoughts and reflections to help guide you on this journey:

Start small. You don't need to spend hours meditating or retreat to a remote cabin in the woods to experience the benefits of quietness. Simply setting aside a few minutes each day to sit quietly, breathe, and reflect can have a profound impact on your well-being.

Practice self-compassion. Embracing quietness can be challenging, and you may face setbacks or obstacles along the way. Remember to be kind and compassionate with yourself, and to celebrate your successes, no matter how small.

Find support. Surround yourself with people who understand and support your journey towards quietness. Seek out communities or groups that share your values and goals, and lean on friends and family who can provide encouragement and accountability.

Be patient. Cultivating a life of quietness is a journey, not a destination. Be patient with yourself, and trust that each step you take towards stillness and solitude is bringing you closer to the peace and fulfillment you seek.

In closing, I would like to offer my heartfelt gratitude to you, the reader, for accompanying me on this journey towards quietness. I hope that the insights and strategies we have explored together in this book have inspired you to embrace stillness and solitude as a powerful tool for self-discovery and personal growth.

Remember that the power of quietness is always within you, waiting to be unlocked. May you find the strength and courage to embrace this power, and to live your life with greater purpose, meaning, and joy.

As you move forward on this journey, I invite you to take a moment to reflect on what you have learned and how you can apply these insights to your life. Perhaps you can set aside time each day for meditation or reflection, or make a commitment to prioritize self-care and self-awareness. Whatever path you choose, remember that the key to unlocking the power of quietness is to stay present, curious, and open to all that life has to offer.

In the end, the journey towards quietness is not just about finding inner peace or personal growth. It is about living a life of purpose and meaning, and creating a world that reflects our deepest values and aspirations. As you embark on this journey, may you be guided by the wisdom and insight that you have gained, and may you find the courage and strength to create a life that truly reflects the power and potential of quietness.

Thank You

As we reach the end of this book, I want to say thanks for reading this book.

I want to get this information out to as many people as possible. If you found this book helpful, I would greatly appreciate you leaving me a review. This helps others find the book as well.

Disclaimer

This document is geared towards providing exact and reliable information in regards to the topic and issue covered. The publication is sold on the idea that the publisher is not required to render an accounting, officially permitted, or otherwise, qualified services. If advice is necessary, legal, financial, medical or professional, a practiced individual in the profession should be ordered.

This information is not presented by a financial or medical practitioner and is for entertainment, educational and informational purposes only. The content is not intended as a substitute for professional medical advice, diagnosis, or treatment. Always seek the advice of your physician or other qualified health care provider with any questions you may have regarding a medical condition. Never disregard professional medical advice or delay in seeking it because of something you have read.

The information provided herein is stated to be truthful and consistent, in that any liability, in terms of inattention or otherwise, by any usage or abuse of any policies, processes, or directions contained within is the solitary and utter responsibility of the recipient reader. Under no circumstances

DISCLAIMER

will any legal responsibility or blame be held against the publisher for any reparation, damages, or monetary loss due to the information herein, either directly or indirectly.